A-Z GUILDFORD

C000082777

CONTENTS

REFERENCE

Motorway	**M25**	**Car Park** (Selected)	**P**
		Park & Ride	**P+**
A Road	A3	**Church or Chapel**	†
B Road	B380	**Fire Station**	■
Dual Carriageway		**Hospital**	**H**
One-way Street		**House Numbers** A & B Roads Only	2 33
Traffic flow on A roads is indicated by a heavy line on the drivers' left		**Information Centre**	**i**
Large Scale Pages Only		**National Grid Reference**	¹50
Restricted Access		**Police Station**	▲
Pedestrianized Road		**Post Office**	★
Track & Footpath		**Toilet** with Facilities for the Disabled	▽
Residential Walkway		**Viewpoint**	☀
Railway	Level Crossing / Station	**Educational Establishment**	⬠
		Hospital or Hospice	⬠
Built-up Area	MILL ST	**Industrial Building**	⬠
		Leisure or Recreational Facility	⬠
Local Authority Boundary		**Place of Interest**	⬠
Postcode Boundary		**Public Building**	⬠
Map Continuation	Large Scale Town Centre	**Shopping Centre or Market**	⬠
	5 / 36	**Other Selected Buildings**	⬠

SCALES

Map Pages 2-35 1:19,000

0	¼	½ Mile
0	250	500	750 Metres

3.33 inches (8.47cm) to 1 mile   5.26 cm to 1 km

Map Page 36 1:9,500

0	⅛	¼ Mile
0	125	250	375 Metres

6.67 inches (16.94cm) to 1 mile   10.53 cm to 1 km

Copyright of Geographers' A-Z Map Company Limited

Head Office :
Fairfield Road, Borough Green, Sevenoaks, Kent TN15 8PP
Telephone: 01732 781000 (Enquiries & Trade Sales)
01732 783422 (Retail Sales)
www.a-zmaps.co.uk

Copyright © Geographers' A-Z Map Co. Ltd.

Ordnance Survey® This product includes mapping data licensed from Ordnance Survey® with the permission of the Controller of Her Majesty's Stationery Office.
© Crown Copyright 2002. All rights reserved. Licence number 100017302

EDITION 2 2002   EDITION 2A* 2003 (part revision)

Every possible care has been taken to ensure that, to the best of our knowledge, the information contained in this atlas is accurate at the date of publication. However, we cannot warrant that our work is entirely error free and whilst we would be grateful to learn of any inaccuracies, we do not accept any responsibility for loss or damage resulting from reliance on information contained in this publication.

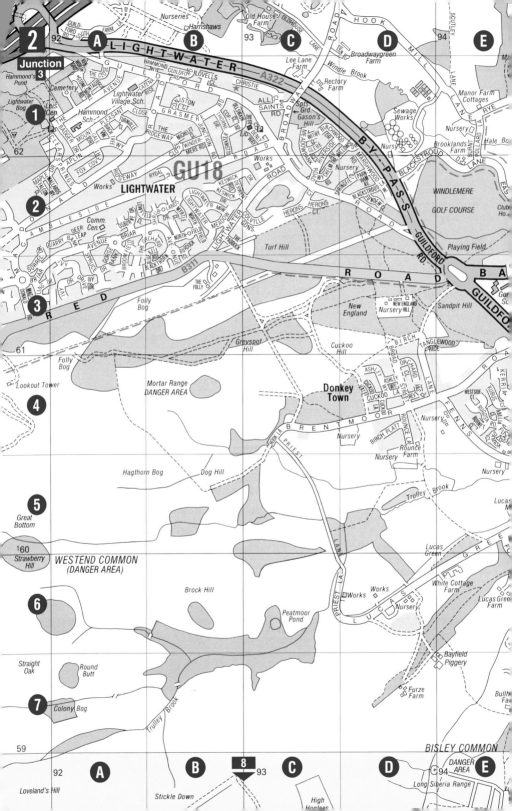

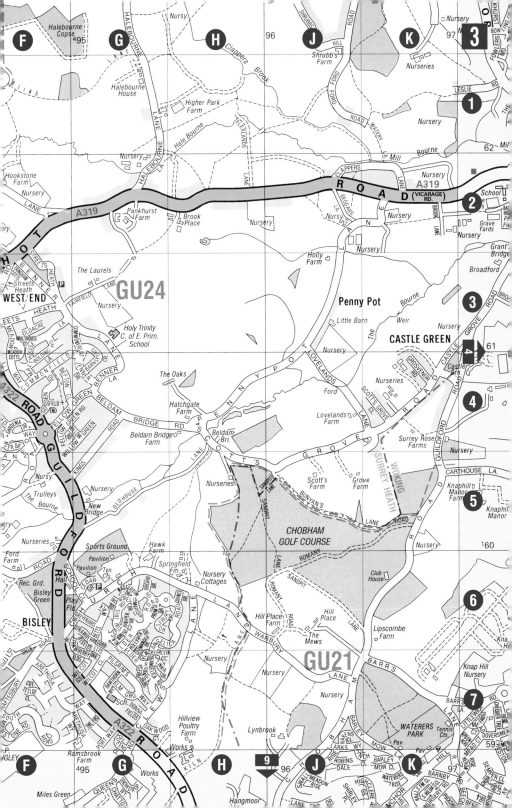

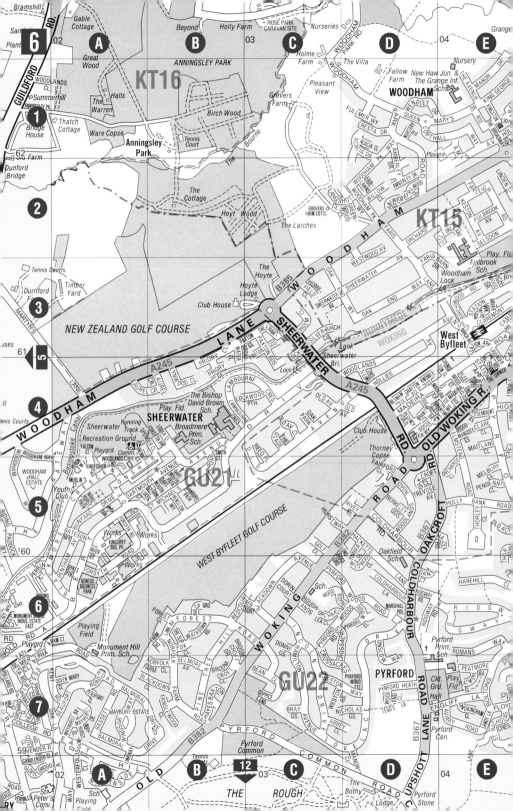

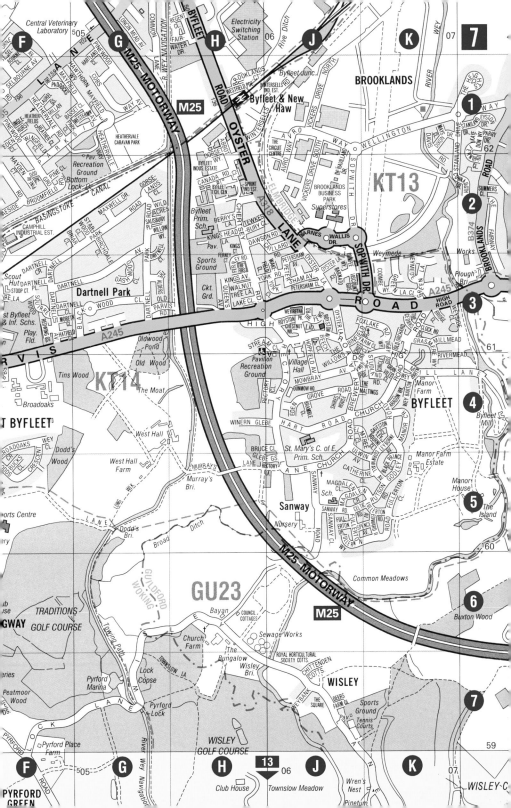

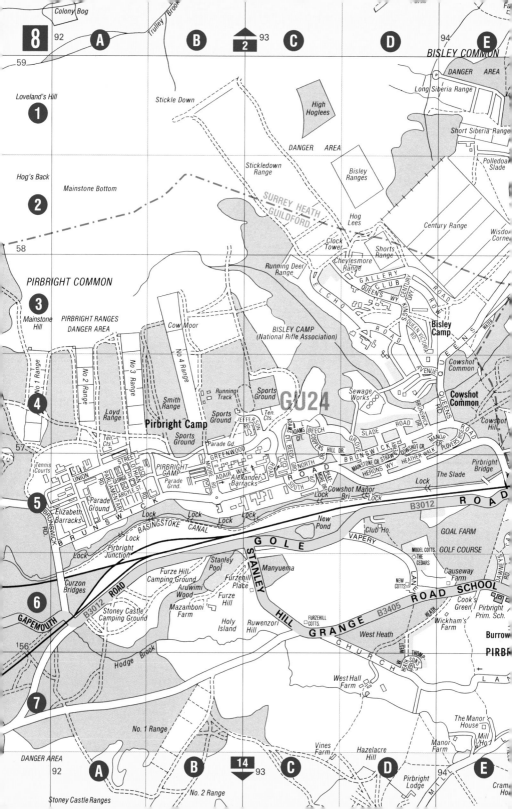

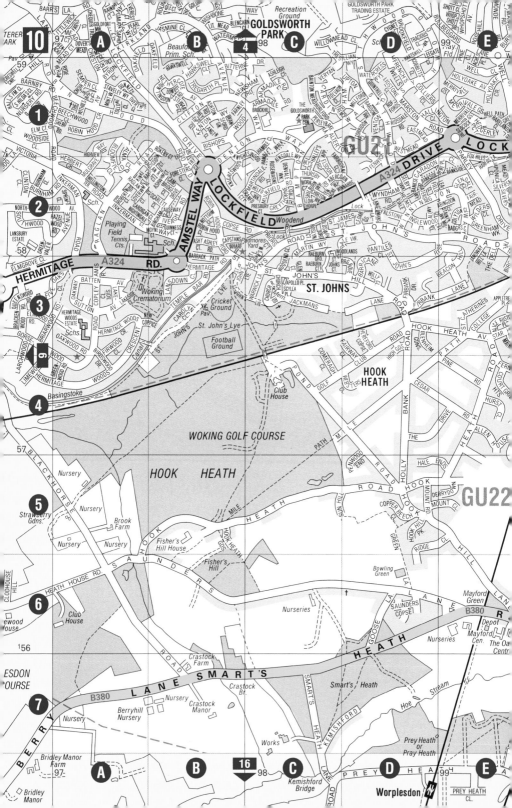

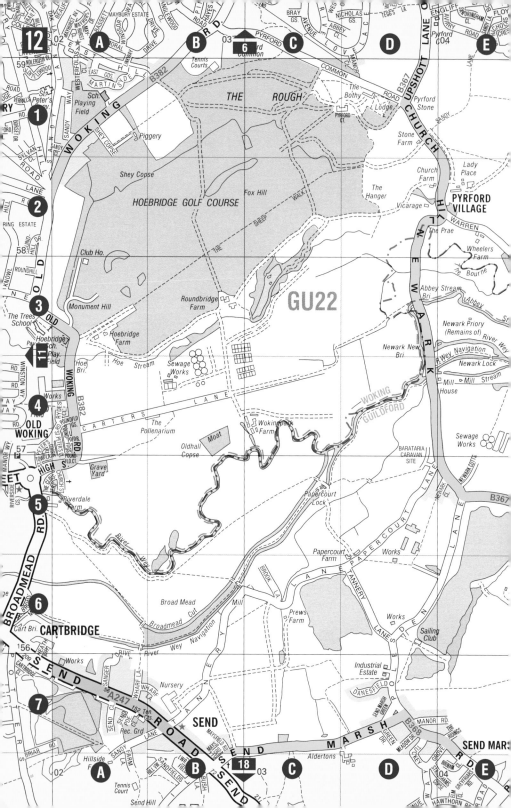

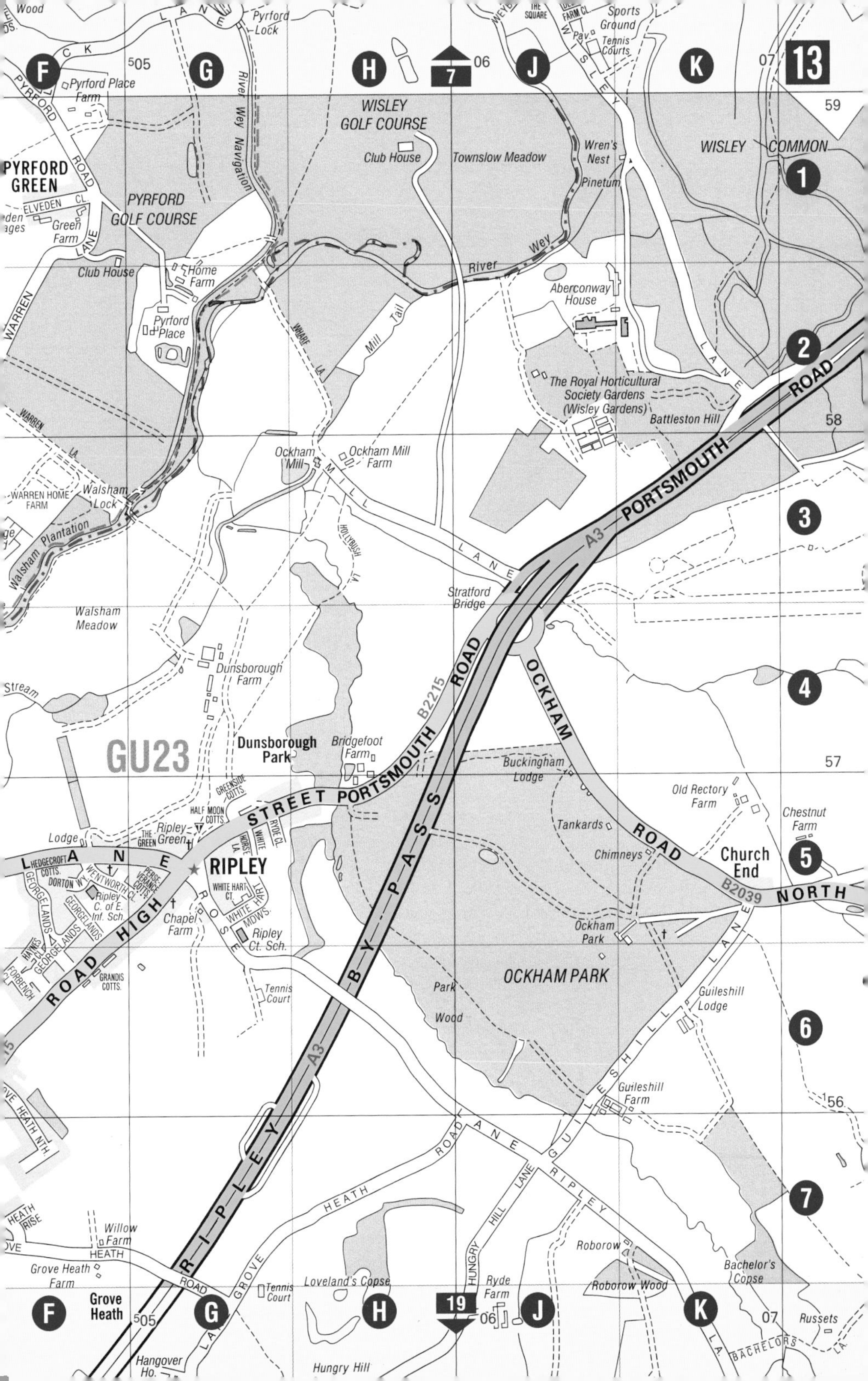

7
19
F G H J K
1 2 3 4 5 6 7
505 06 07
59 58 57 56
WISLEY GOLF COURSE
Club House
Townslow Meadow
Wren's Nest
Pinetum
WISLEY COMMON
Sports Ground
Tennis Courts
Pav.
Pyrford Lock
Pyrford Place Farm
PYRFORD GREEN
PYRFORD GOLF COURSE
ELVEDEN CL.
Green Farm
Club House
Home Farm
Pyrford Place
River Wey Navigation
River Wey
Aberconway House
The Royal Horticultural Society Gardens (Wisley Gardens)
Battleston Hill
PORTSMOUTH ROAD
A3
Mill Tail
WHARF LA.
Ockham Mill
Ockham Mill Farm
MILL LANE
HOLLYBUSH LA.
WARREN LANE
WARREN HOME FARM
Walsham Lock
Walsham Plantation
Walsham Meadow
Stratford Bridge
Dunsborough Farm
Dunsborough Park
Stream
GU23
Bridgefoot Farm
B2215
OCKHAM ROAD
Buckingham Lodge
Tankards
Chimneys
Old Rectory Farm
Chestnut Farm
Church End
B2039 NORTH
PORTSMOUTH ROAD
STREET
GREENSIDE COTTS.
HALF MOON COTTS.
Ripley Green
THE GREEN
Lodge
HIGH ROAD
LANE
HEDGECROFT COTTS.
DORTON WY.
WENTWORTH CL.
PERSEVERANCE COTTS.
RIPLEY
WHITE HART CT.
WHITE HART MDWS.
HORSE LA.
WHITE
RYDE CL.
Ripley C. of E. Inf. Sch.
GEORGELANDS
Chapel Farm
ROSE
Ripley Ct. Sch.
HAYNES
FORBENCH CL.
GRANDIS COTTS.
Tennis Court
RIPLEY BY PASS
Ockham Park
OCKHAM PARK
Park Wood
Guileshill Lodge
GUILESHILL LANE
Guileshill Farm
RIPLEY LANE
HUNGRY HILL LANE
HEATH ROAD
GROVE HEATH NTH
HEATH RISE
Willow Farm
GROVE HEATH ROAD
Grove Heath Farm
Grove Heath
GROVE LA.
Tennis Court
Loveland's Copse
Roborow
Roborow Wood
Ryde Farm
Bachelor's Copse
Russets
BACHELORS LA.
LA.
Hangover Ho.
Hungry Hill

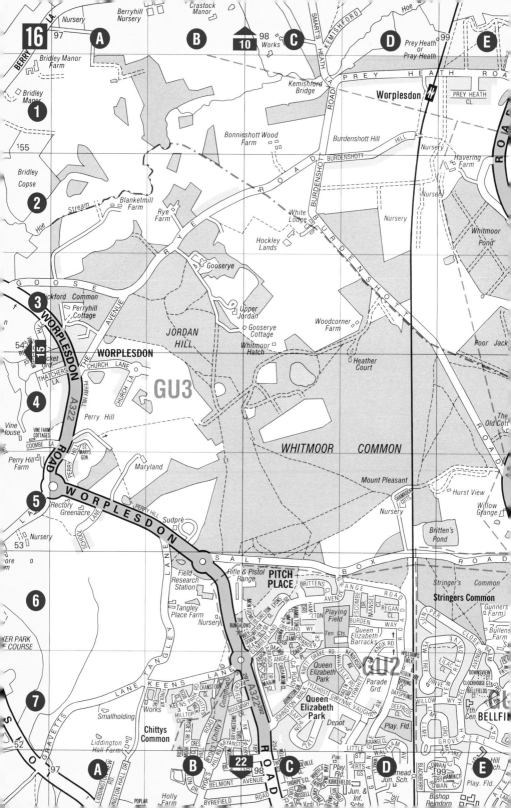

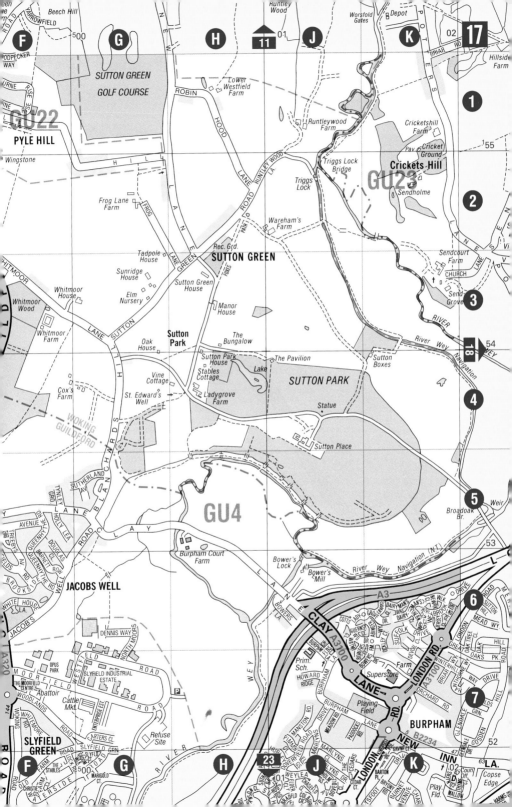

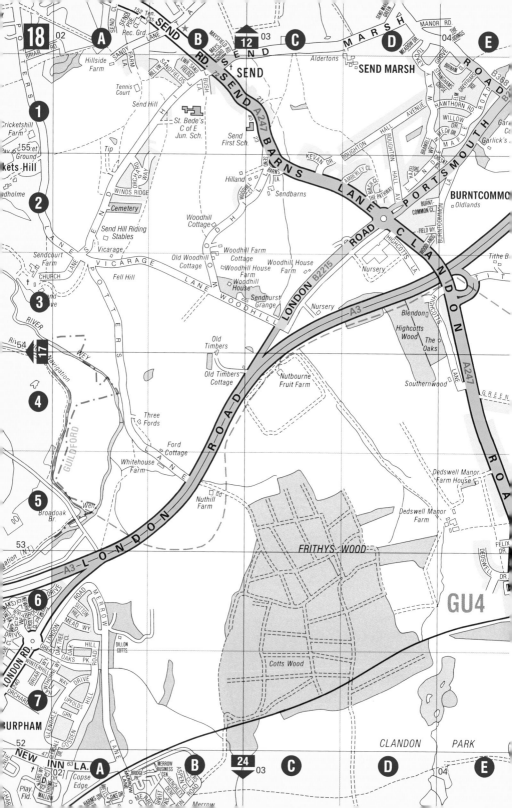

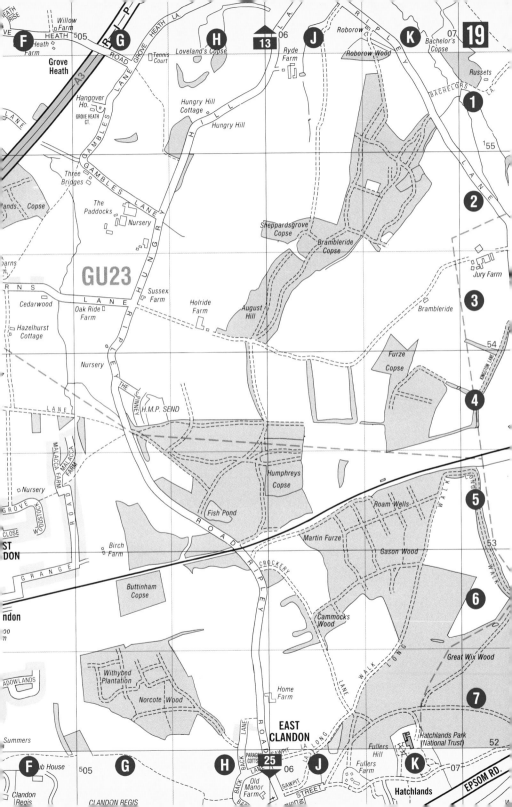

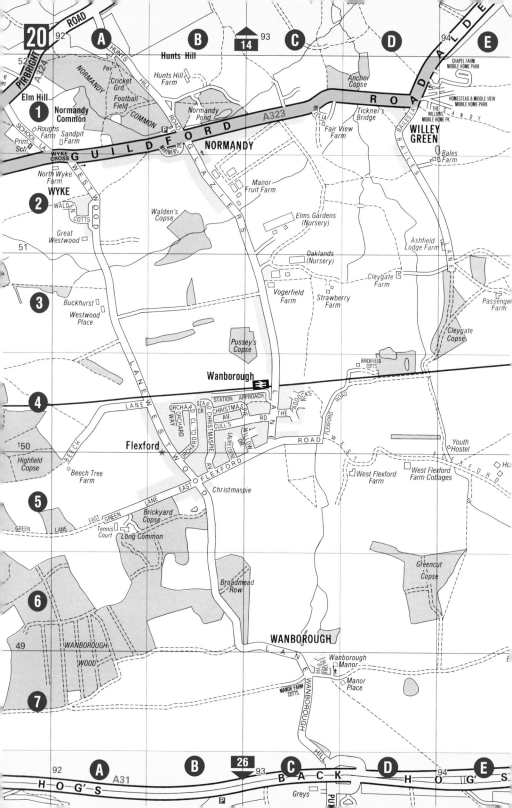

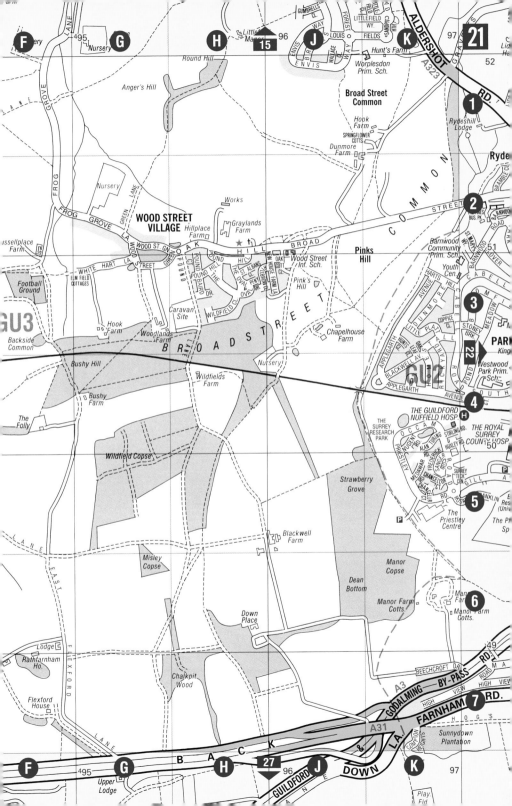

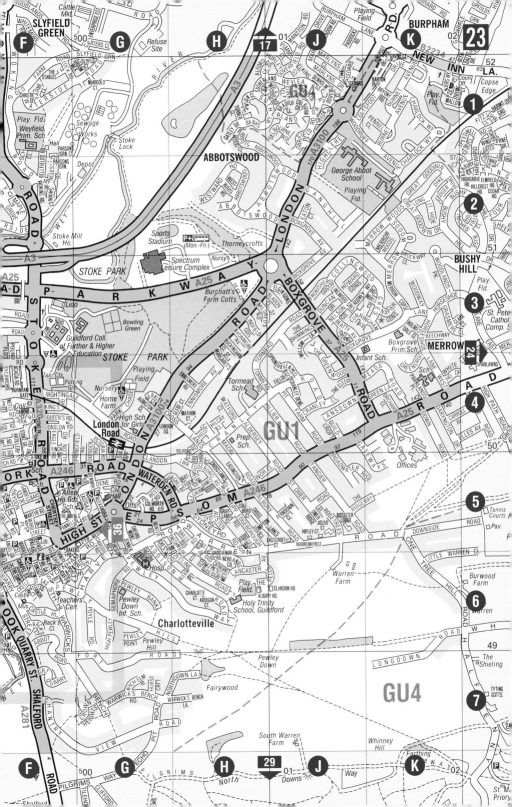

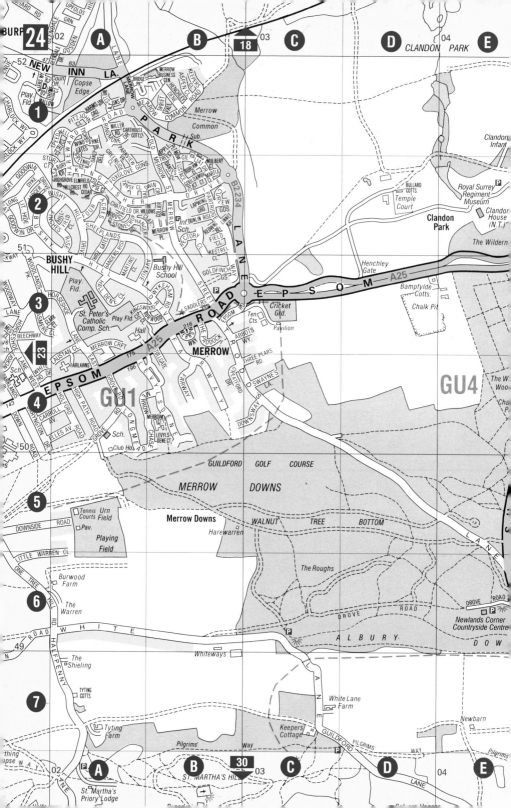

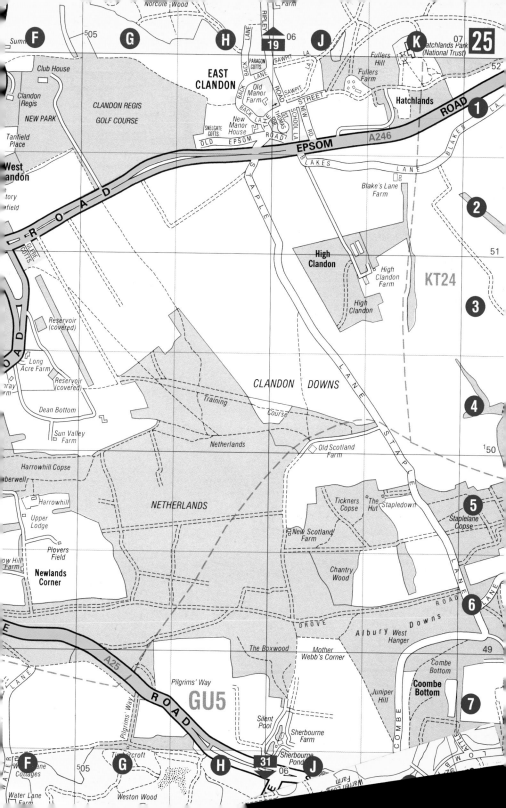

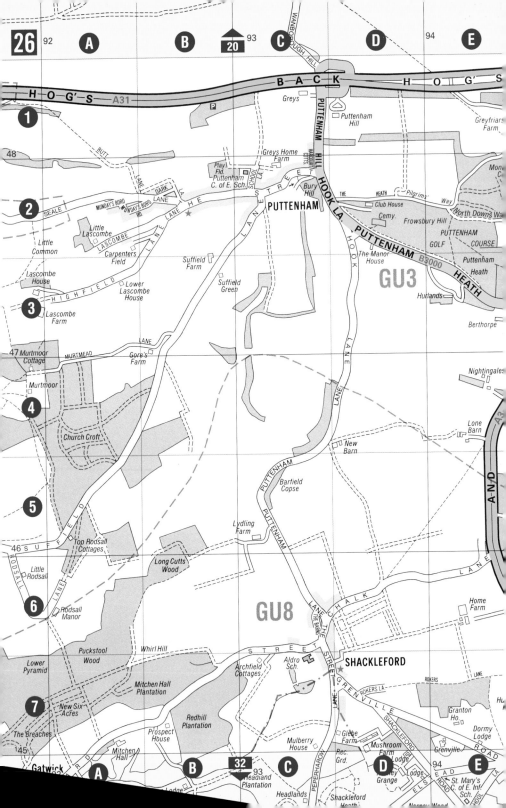

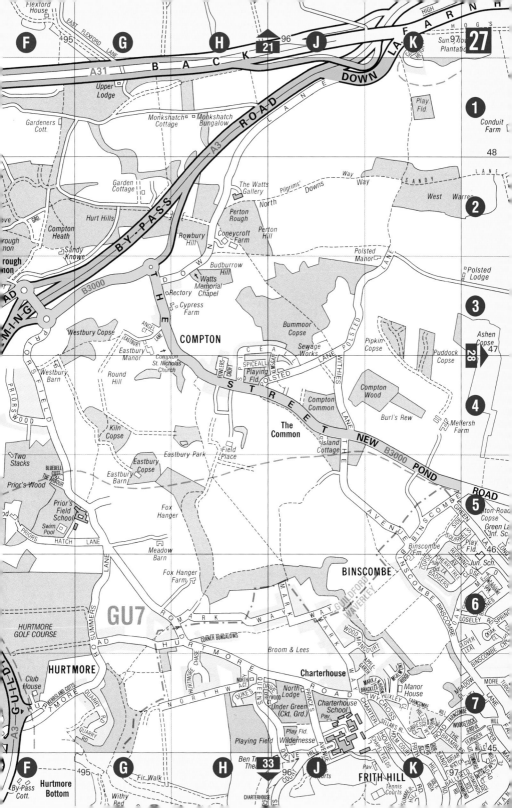

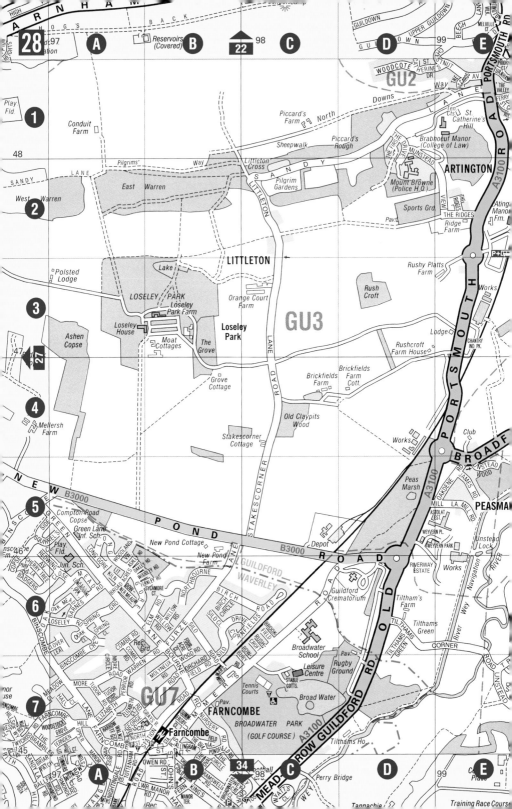

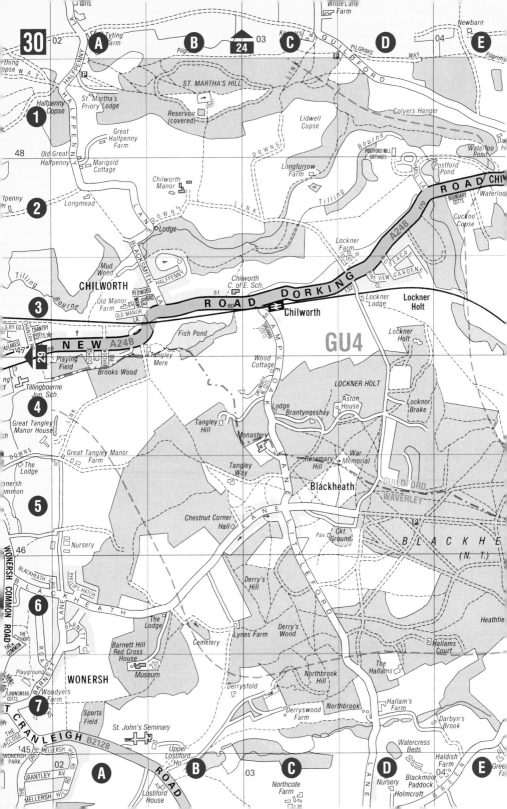

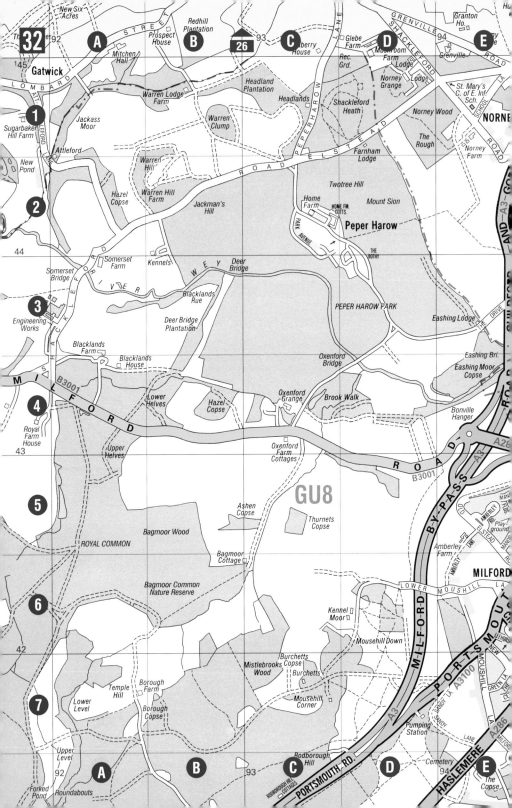

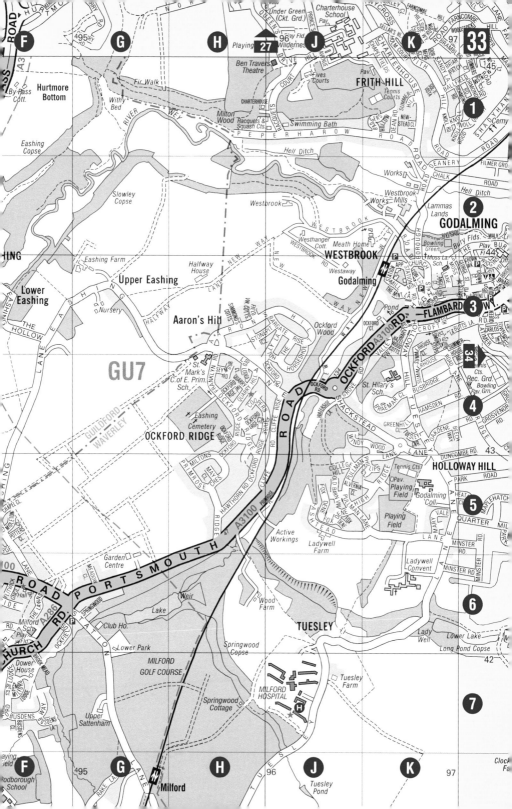

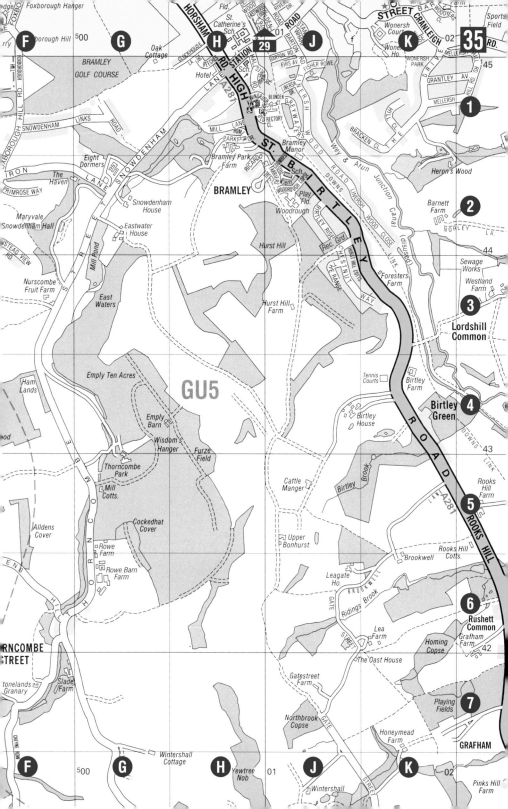

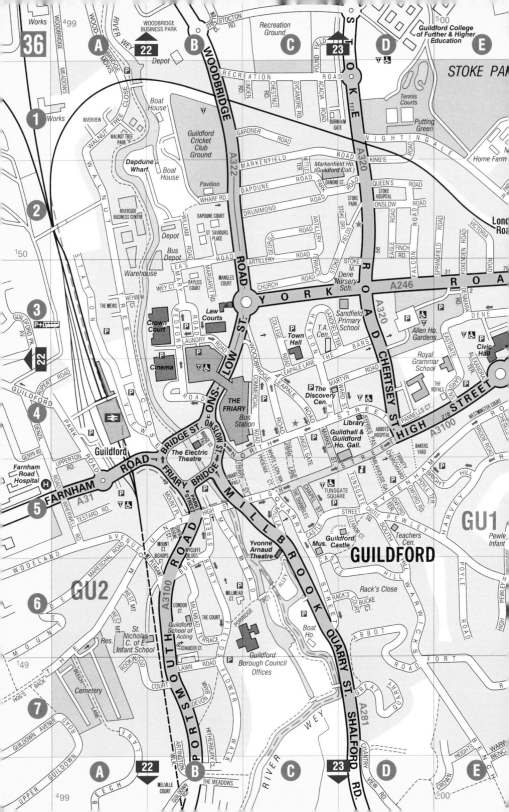

INDEX

Including Streets, Places & Areas, Hospitals & Hospices, Industrial Estates,
Selected Flats & Walkways and Selected Places of Interest.

HOW TO USE THIS INDEX

. Each street name is followed by its Posttown or Postal Locality and then by its map reference; e.g. Aaron's Hill *G'ming* ....3H **33** is in the Godalming Posttown and is to be found in square 3H on page **33**. The page number being shown in bold type.

. A strict alphabetical order is followed in which Av., Rd., St., etc. (though abbreviated) are read in full and as part of the street name; e.g. Ash Gro. appears after Ashenden Rd. but before Ashley Ct.

. Streets and a selection of flats and walkways too small to be shown on the maps, appear in the index in *Italics* with the thoroughfare to which it is connected shown in brackets; e.g. *Allden Cotts. G'ming ....3H **33** (off Aaron's Hill)*

. Places and areas are shown in the index in **blue type** and the map reference is to the actual map square in which the town centre or area is located and not to the place name shown on the map; e.g. **Albury Heath 4H 31**

. An example of a selected place of interest is British Red Cross Mus. & Archives 7A 30

. An example of a hospital or hospice is CHASE CHILDREN'S HOSPICE 2E 28

. Map references shown in brackets; e.g. Abbot Rd. *Guild* ....6F **23** (6D **36**) refer to entries that also appear on the large scale page **36**.

GENERAL ABBREVIATIONS

All : Alley	Ct : Court	Lit : Little	Rd : Road
App : Approach	Cres : Crescent	Lwr : Lower	Shop : Shopping
Arc : Arcade	Cft : Croft	Mc : Mac	S : South
Av : Avenue	Dri : Drive	Mnr : Manor	Sq : Square
Bk : Back	E : East	Mans : Mansions	Sta : Station
Boulevd : Boulevard	Embkmt : Embankment	Mkt : Market	St : Street
Bri : Bridge	Est : Estate	Mdw : Meadow	Ter : Terrace
B'way : Broadway	Fld : Field	M : Mews	Trad : Trading
Bldgs : Buildings	Gdns : Gardens	Mt : Mount	Up : Upper
Bus : Business	Gth : Garth	Mus : Museum	Va : Vale
Cvn : Caravan	Ga : Gate	N : North	Vw : View
Cen : Centre	Gt : Great	Pal : Palace	Vs : Villas
Chu : Church	Grn : Green	Pde : Parade	Vis : Visitors
Chyd : Churchyard	Gro : Grove	Pk : Park	Wlk : Walk
Circ : Circle	Ho : House	Pas : Passage	W : West
Cir : Circus	Ind : Industrial	Pl : Place	Yd : Yard
Clo : Close	Info : Information	Quad : Quadrant	
Comn : Common	Junct : Junction	Res : Residential	
Cotts : Cottages	La : Lane	Ri : Rise	

POSTTOWN AND POSTAL LOCALITY ABBREVIATIONS

Alb : Albury	*G'ming* : Godalming	*Ott* : Ottershaw	*Wanb* : Wanborough
Art : Artington	*Gray* : Grayshott	*P'mrsh* : Peasmarsh	*W Byf* : West Byfleet
Bisl : Bisley	*Guild* : Guildford	*Pep H* : Peper Harow	*W Cla* : West Clandon
B'hth : Blackheath	*Hamb* : Hambledon	*Pirb* : Pirbright	*W End* : West End
Brmly : Bramley	*Hors* : Horsell	*Pyr* : Pyrford	*W Hor* : West Horsley
Bro I : Brooklands Industrial Estate	*Hurt* : Hurtmore	*P'ham* : Puttenham	*Wey* : Weybridge
Bro P : Brooklands Industrial Park	*Hyde* : Hydestile	*Rip* : Ripley	*W'sham* : Windlesham
Brkwd : Brookwood	*Jac* : Jacob's Well	*Seale* : Seale	*Wis* : Wisley
Burp : Burpham	*Kingf* : Kingfield	*Send* : Send	*Witl* : Witley
Busb : Busbridge	*Knap* : Knaphill	*Shack* : Shackleford	*Wok* : Woking
Byfl : Byfleet	*Light* : Lightwater	*Shalf* : Shalford	*Won* : Wonersh
Cher : Chertsey	*Lwr E* : Lower Eashing	*Sham G* : Shamley Green	*Wdhm* : Woodham
Chil : Chilworth	*Mayf* : Mayford	*Sheer* : Sheerwater	*Wood S* : Wood Street Village
Chob : Chobham	*Milf* : Milford	*Shere* : Shere	*Wmly* : Wormley
Comp : Compton	*New H* : New Haw	*Sly I* : Slyfield Industrial Estate	*Worp* : Worplesdon
E Clan : East Clandon	*Norm* : Normandy	*St J* : St Johns	*Worp H* : Worplesdon Hill
E Hor : East Horsley	*Ock* : Ockham	*Sur R* : Surrey Research Park	
Elst : Elstead	*Old Wok* : Old Woking	*Sut G* : Sutton Green	
Farnc : Farncombe	*Onsl* : Onslow Village	*Thur* : Thursley	

A

	Acacia Rd. *Guild* 4F **23** (1C **36**)	Aldersey Rd. *Guild* 4H **23**	Alpha Rd. *Wok* 7K **5**
	Acer Dri. *W End* 4F **3**	Aldershot Rd. *Norm & Guild* ...7E **14**	Alresford Rd. *Guild* 5C **22**
Aaron's Hill.............3H **33**	Achilles Pl. *Wok* 1E **10**	Aldershot Rd. *Pirb*............4D **14**	Alterton Clo. *Wok* 1C **10**
Aaron's Hill. *G'ming* 3H **33**	Acorn Gro. *Wok* 5G **11**	Alders, The. *W Byf* 3G **7**	Alvernia Clo. *G'ming* 5J **33**
Abbey Clo. *Wok*..............7C **6**	Adair Wlk. *Brkwd* 5B **8**	Alexandra Gdns. *Knap* 2J **9**	Alwyne Ct. *Wok*..............7G **5**
Abbey Rd. *Wok* 1E **10**	Adams Cft. *Brkwd*.............4C **8**	Alexandra Pl. *Guild* 6H **23**	Ambassador Theatre Group, The.
Abbot Clo. *Byfl* 1H **7**	Addison Ct. *Guild* 6H **23**	Alexandra Ter. *Guild* 5G **23** (3E **36**)	.................................1G **11**
Abbot Rd. *Guild* 6F **23** (6D **36**)	Addison Rd. *Guild*............6G **23**	Alford Clo. *Guild* 1H **23**	Amberley Clo. *Send*..........2D **18**
Abbot's Clo. *Guild* 7A **22**	Addison Rd. *Wok*.............1H **11**	Alice Ruston Pl. *Wok*..........3E **10**	Amberley Dri. *Wdhm*..........1D **6**
Abbotsford Clo. *Wok*..........1J **11**	Admirals Ct. *Guild*............3K **23**	Alison Clo. *Wok*...............6G **5**	(in two parts)
Abbots Hospital. *Guild* 4D **36**	Admiral's Rd. *Pirb*............3A **14**	Allden Cotts. *G'ming* 3H **33**	Amberley La. *Milf* 6E **32**
Abbots Way. *Guild*............3B **24**	Agraria Rd. *Guild*.............5D **22**	(off Aaron's Hill)	Amberley Rd. *Milf* 5E **32**
Abbotswood...............2H **23**	Ainsdale Way. *Wok* 2C **10**	Alldens Hill. *G'ming & Brmly*...6F **35**	Ambleside. *G'ming* 2C **34**
Abbotswood. *Guild*............2H **23**	Alanbrooke Clo. *Knap* 2J **9**	Alldens La. *G'ming* 5D **34**	Ambleside Rd. *Light* 2A **2**
Abbotswood Clo. *Guild*........1H **23**	Alan Turing Rd. *Sur R* 4K **21**	Allen Ho. Pk. *Wok*............4E **10**	Amis Av. *New H*................1E **6**
Abelia Clo. *W End* 4E **2**	Albert Dri. *Wok* 6A **6**	Allingham Ct. *G'ming* 7B **28**	Amis Rd. *Wok*................3A **10**
Abercorn Way. *Wok*...........2C **10**	Albion Ho. *Wok* 1H **11**	Allingham Rd. *Wok*............2D **10**	Amstel Way. *Wok* 2B **10**
Abingdon Clo. *Wok* 2E **10**	Albury. 2F **31**	All Saints Rd. *Light* 1C **2**	Anchor Cres. *Knap* 1K **9**
Abinger Way. *Guild* 6K **17**	**Albury Heath**...............4H **31**	Alma Clo. *Knap*...............1A **10**	Anchor Hill. *Knap* 1K **9**
Acacia Av. *Wok* 4F **11**	Albury Ho. *Guild*.............6H **23**	Almond Av. *Wok* 5F **11**	Angel Ct. *Comp*...............3G **27**
Acacia Clo. *Wdhm*.............1D **6**	Albury Park. 3J **31**	Almond Clo. *Guild* 1F **23**	Angel Ct. *G'ming*..............3K **33**
Acacia Dri. *Wdhm* 1D **6**	Albury Pk. *Alb* 2J **31**	Almsgate. *Comp* 4J **27**	Angel Ga. *Guild*......5F **23** (4C **36**)
	Albury Rd. *Guild* 5H **23**	Alpha Rd. *Chob*................1B **4**	Angelica Rd. *Bisl*...............6G **3**

Angelica Rd.—Brookfield

Angelica Rd. *Guild* 7C 16
Annandale Rd. *Guild* 6D 22
Anningsley Park. 1A 6
Anningsley Pk. *Ott.* 1K 5
Anston Ct. *Guild* 4A 22
Anthonys. 3J 5
Apers Av. *Wok* 5H 11
Aplin Way. *Light* 2A 2
Apollo Pl. *St J* 3C 10
Applegarth. *G'ming* 7K 27
Applegarth Av. *Guild* 4K 21
Appletree Clo. *G'ming* 5B 34
Appletree Ct. *Guild* 1B 24
Appletrees Pl. *Wok* 3E 10
Aprilwood Clo. *Wdhm* 2D 6
Aragon Wlk. *Byfl* 4K 7
Aram Ct. *Wok* 6A 6
Arbour, The. *Hurt* 5F 27
Ardmore Av. *Guild* 2D 22
Ardmore Ho. *Guild* 2D 22
Ardmore Way. *Guild* 2D 22
Arethusa Way. *Bisl* 7F 3
Argyle St. *Brkwd* 5A 8
Armadale Rd. *Wok* 1C 10
Arnold Rd. *Wok* 6K 5
Arreton Mead. *Hors* 5H 5
Arthur's Bri. Rd. *Wok* 1E 10
Arthur's Bri. Wharf. *Wok* 1F 11
Artillery Rd. *Guild* 5F 23 (3C 36)
Artillery Ter. *Guild* 4F 23 (2C 36)
Artington. 2E 28
Artington Wlk. *Guild* 7E 22 (7B 36)
Ashbury Cres. *Guild* 2A 24
Ash Clo. *Pyr* 6E 6
Ash Clo. *Wok* 4G 11
Ashcroft. *Shalf* 4G 29
Ashenden Rd. *Guild* 4B 22
Ash Gro. *Guild* 4C 22
Ashley Ct. *Wok* 2B 10
Ashley Gdns. *Shalf* 4H 29
Ashley Ho. *G'ming* 6A 28
Ashley Rd. *Wok* 2B 10
Ashley Way. *W End* 4D 2
Ash Rd. *Pirb* 3F 15
Ash Rd. *Wok* 4F 11
Ashtead La. *G'ming* 5J 33
Ashton Rd. *Wok* 1B 10
Ashwindham Ct. *Wok* 2B 10
Ashwood Pk. *Wok* 2J 11
Ashwood Rd. *Wok* 2H 11
Ashworth Pl. *Guild* 4B 22
Aspen Clo. *Guild* 1B 24
Astolat Est. *P'mrsh* 5E 28
Atherton Clo. *Shalf* 3G 29
Atkins Clo. *Wok* 2C 10
Attleford La. *Shack* 1A 32
August La. *Alb* 7H 31
Austen Rd. *Guild* 5H 23
Avenue de Cagny. *Pirb* 6F 9
Avenue, The. *Chob* 1C 4
Avenue, The. *Comp & G'ming* 4J 27
Avenue, The. *G'ming* 5A 34
Avenue, The. *Light* 1A 2
Avenue, The. *New H* 1E 6
Avenue, The. *Worp* 4A 16
Aviary Rd. *Wok* 7E 6
Avington Clo. *Guild* 4G 23
Avonmead. *Wok* 2E 10
Avonmore Av. *Guild* 3H 23
Avro Way. *Bro P* 1J 7
Azalea Ct. *Wok* 3F 11

B

Bachelors La. *Ock* 1K 19
Back La. *E Clan* 1H 25
Bk. of High St. *Chob* 2A 4
Baden Rd. *Guild* 2C 22
Badger Clo. *Guild* 1D 22
Badger Dri. *Light* 1A 2
Badgers Clo. *G'ming* 6K 27
Badgers Clo. *Wok* 2E 10
Badgers Cross. *Milf* 6F 33
Badgers Hollow. *G'ming* 1K 33
Badger Wlk. *Norm* 5C 14
Bagshot Rd. *Knap & Worp H* 2H 9
Bagshot Rd. *W End & Chob* 3E 2
Bailes La. *Norm* 1D 20
Baillie Rd. *Guild* 5H 23
Bainton Mead. *Wok* 1C 10
Baird Dri. *Wood S* 3H 21
Baker's Yd. *Guild* 5F 23 (4D 36)
Baldwin Cres. *Guild* 2A 24
Balfour Av. *Wok* 6G 11
Ballfield Rd. *G'ming* 1K 33
Balmoral Dri. *Wok* 7A 6
Bampton Way. *Wok* 2C 10
Banders Ri. *Guild* 3A 24
Bankside. *Wok* 2D 10
(in three parts)
Banks Way. *Guild* 1H 23
Bannister's Rd. *Guild* 6B 22
Barataria Cvn. Site. *Rip* 4D 12
Bardon Wlk. *Wok* 1D 10
Bargate Ct. *Guild* 4A 22
Bargate Ri. *G'ming* 3J 33
Barley Mow Clo. *Knap* 1K 9
Barley Mow La. *Knap* 7J 3
Barnard Ct. *Wok* 2A 10
Barnato Clo. *W Byf* 3J 7
Barnby Rd. *Knap* 1K 9
Barnes Rd. *G'ming* 6A 28
Barnes Wallis Dri. *Wey* 2J 7
Barnett Clo. *Won* 6A 30
Barnett La. *Won* 7K 29
Barnett Row. *Guild* 6F 17
Barnmead. *Chob* 1B 4
Barnsbury Farm Est. *Wok* 4F 11
Barnsford Cres. *W End* 4G 3
Barns, The. *Shack* 6C 26
Barnwood Clo. *Guild* 2A 22
Barnwood Rd. *Guild* 3A 22
Barrack Path. *Wok* 3B 10
Barrack Rd. *Guild* 2C 22
Barrens Brae. *Wok* 2J 11
Barrens Clo. *Wok* 3J 11
Barrens Pk. *Wok* 2J 11
Barricane. *Wok* 3D 10
Barr's La. *Knap* 7K 3
(in two parts)
Bars, The. *Guild* 5F 23 (3C 36)
Barton Pl. *Guild* 1K 23
Barton Rd. *Brmly* 7J 29
Basset Clo. *New H* 1F 7
Bassett Rd. *Wok* 7A 6
Bateson Way. *Wok* 5A 6
Batten Av. *Wok* 3A 10
Battersea Ct. *Guild* 4C 22
Bayliss Ct. *Guild* 5E 22 (3B 36)
Beacon Hill. *Wok* 3E 10
Beaconsfield Rd. *Wok* 4H 11
Beatty Av. *Guild* 3J 23
Beaufort Clo. *Wok* 7A 6
Beaufort Rd. *Wok* 7A 6
Beavers Clo. *Guild* 3A 22
Beckingham Rd. *Guild* 2C 22
Bedford Clo. *Wok* 6E 4
Bedford Rd. *Guild* 5E 22 (3B 36)
Bedser Clo. *Wok* 7J 5
Beech Clo. *Byfl* 3J 7
Beechcroft Dri. *Guild* 7K 21
Beech Dri. *Rip* 1E 18
Beeches, The. *Brmly* 1H 35
Beech Gdns. *Wok* 6G 5
Beech Gro. *Brkwd* 4C 8
(in two parts)
Beech Gro. *Guild* 4B 22
Beech Gro. *Mayf* 7F 11
Beech Hill. *Wok* 7F 11
Beech La. *Guild* 7E 22 (7A 36)
(in two parts)
Beech La. *Norm* 5A 20
Beechlawn. *Guild* 5H 23
Beechvale. Wok 2H 11
(off Fairview Av.)
Beech Way. *G'ming* 4K 33
Beechway. *Guild* 3K 23
Beechwood Clo. *Knap* 1A 10
Beechwood Rd. *Knap* 1A 10
Beggars La. *Chob* 2J 3
Beldam Bri. Rd. *Chob* 4G 3
Belgrave Mnr. *Wok* 3G 11
Bellfields. 7E 16
Bellfields Ct. *Guild* 7E 16
Bellfields Rd. *Guild* 2F 23
Belmont Av. *Guild* 1B 22
Belmore Av. *Wok* 7B 6
Belvedere Clo. *Guild* 2D 22
Benbrick Rd. *Guild* 5C 22
Benner La. *W End* 3F 3
Bennett Way. *W Cla* 6E 18
Bentham Av. *Wok* 6A 6
Benwell Rd. *Brkwd* 3F 9
Berberis Clo. *Guild* 2E 22
(in two parts)
Bergenia Ct. *W End* 4E 2
Berkeley Gdns. *W Byf* 5D 6
Berkley Ct. *Guild* 4G 23
Berry La. *Worp* 2J 15
(in two parts)
Berry's La. *Byfl* 2H 7
Beta Rd. *Chob* 1B 4
Beta Rd. *Wok* 7K 5
Bethany Pl. *Wok* 2F 11
Binfield Rd. *Byfl* 3J 7
Bingham Dri. *Wok* 2B 10
Binscombe. 6K 27
Binscombe. *G'ming* 5K 27
Binscombe Cres. *G'ming* 7A 28
Binscombe La. *G'ming* 6K 27
Birchanger. *G'ming* 3A 34
Birch Circ. *G'ming* 6B 28
Birch Clo. *Send* 2D 18
Birch Clo. *Wok* 3E 10
Birchdale Clo. *W Byf* 2G 7
Birches, The. *Wok* 2H 11
Birch Gro. *Guild* 1E 22
Birch Gro. *Wok* 6B 6
Birch La. *W End* 3D 2
Birch Platt. *W End* 4D 2
Birch Rd. *G'ming* 6B 28
Birch Tree Vw. *Light* 1A 2
Birch Wlk. *W Byf* 3E 6
Birchwood Dri. *Light* 1C 2
Birchwood Dri. *W Byf* 3E 6
Birchwood Rd. *W Byf* 3E 6
Birdsgrove. *Knap* 2H 9
Birdswood Dri. *Wok* 3A 10
Birnam Clo. *Rip* 1E 18
Birtley Green. 4K 35
Birtley Ri. *Brmly* 2J 35
Birtley Rd. *Brmly* 2J 35
Bishops Ct. *Guild* 5B 36
Bishops Wood. *Wok* 1B 10
Bisley. 6F 3
Bisley Camp. 3D 8
Bisley Grn. *Bisl* 7F 3
Bitterne Dri. *Wok* 1B 10
Blackberry Clo. *Guild* 1D 22
Blackbridge Rd. *Wok* 3F 11
Blackburn Way. *G'ming* 2B 34
Blackdown Av. *Wok* 6C 6
Blackdown Clo. *Wok* 7A 6
Blackheath. 5C 30
Blackheath 5D 30
Blackheath Gro. *Won* 6K 29
Blackheath La. *Alb* 5F 31
Blackheath La. *Won & B'hth* 6K 29
Blackhorse Rd. *Wok* 4K 9
Blackmore Cres. *Wok* 6A 6
Blackness La. *Wok* 3G 11
Black Prince Clo. *Byfl* 5K 7
Blacksmith La. *Chil* 2A 30
Blackstroud La. E. *Light* 2D 2
Blackstroud La. W. *Light* 2D 2
Blackthorn Dri. *Light* 3B 2
Blackthorn Pl. *Guild* 1E 22
Blackwell Av. *Guild* 4K 21
Blackwood Clo. *W Byf* 3G 7
Bladon Clo. *Guild* 3J 23
Blakes La. *E Clan & W Hor* 2J 25
Blanchards Hill. *Guild* 5G 17
Blandford Clo. *Wok* 1K 11
Blencarn Clo. *Wok* 7B 4
Blenheim Clo. *W Byf* 4D 6
Blenheim Gdns. *Wok* 3D 10
Blewfield. *G'ming* 5B 34
Blind La. *W End* 1F 3
Bloomfield Clo. *Knap* 1A 10
Bloomsbury Ct. Guild 6H 23
(off St Lukes Sq.)
Bluebell Cottage. *Comp* 5F 27
Bluebell Ct. *Wok* 3F 11
Bluebell Ri. *Light* 3B 2
Blunden Ct. *Brmly* 1J 35
Board School Rd. *Wok* 7H 5
Bolding Ho. La. *W End* 4F 3
Boltons Clo. *Wok* 7E 6
Boltons La. *Wok* 7E 6
Bonners Clo. *Wok* 6H 11
Bonsey Clo. *Wok* 5G 11
Bonsey La. *Wok* 5G 11
Bonseys La. *Chob* 1H 5
Borough Rd. *G'ming* 2K 33
Bothy, The. *Pep H* 2D 32
Boughton Hall Av. *Send* 1D 18
Boundary Bus. Cen., The. *Wok* 6J 5
Boundary Cotts. *Chil* 2E 30
Boundary Rd. *Wok* 7J 5
Boundary Way. *Wok* 6J 5
Bourne Clo. *Chil* 3K 29
Bourne Clo. *W Byf* 4F 7
Bourne Rd. *G'ming* 6B 28
Bourne Way. *Wok* 6F 11
Bower Ct. *Wok* 7K 5
Bowers Clo. *Guild* 7J 17
Bowers Farm Dri. *Guild* 7J 17
Bowers La. *Guild* 6J 17
Bowling Grn. Rd. *Chob* 1A 4
Boxgrove Av. *Guild* 2J 23
Boxgrove La. *Guild* 3J 23
Boxgrove Rd. *Guild* 3J 23
Bracken Clo. *Wok* 2H 11
Bracken Clo. *Won* 1J 35
Brackendene Clo. *Wok* 6J 5
Brackenlea. *G'ming* 7K 27
Bracken Way. *Chob* 1B 4
Bracken Way. *Guild* 2A 22
Brackenwood Rd. *Wok* 3K 9
Bradfield Clo. *Guild* 1J 23
Bradfield Clo. *Wok* 2G 11
Braemar Clo. *G'ming* 4K 33
Braeside. *New H* 2F 7
Bramble Clo. *Guild* 2A 22
Brambledene Clo. *Wok* 2E 10
Brambles Pk. *Brmly* 1H 35
Brambles, The. *G'ming* 7K 27
Bramble Way. *Rip* 1D 18
Bramley. 1H 35
Bramley Bus. Cen. Brmly 7H 29
(off Station Rd.)
Bramswell Rd. *G'ming* 1B 34
Brantwood Clo. *W Byf* 4E 6
Brantwood Ct. W Byf 4D 6
(off Brantwood Dri.)
Brantwood Dri. *W Byf* 4D 6
Brantwood Gdns. *W Byf* 4D 6
Bray Gdns. *Wok* 7C 6
Bray Rd. *Guild* 5D 22
Brentmoor Rd. *W End* 4C 2
Brewery La. *Byfl* 4J 7
Brewery Rd. *Wok* 1F 11
Briar Av. *Light* 3A 2
Briar Clo. *W Byf* 2F 7
Briar Patch. *G'ming* 1K 33
Briar Rd. *Send* 1K 17
Briar Wlk. *W Byf* 3E 6
Briar Way. *Guild* 7K 17
Briarwood Rd. *Wok* 3K 9
Brickfield Cotts. *Norm* 4D 20
Bridge Barn La. *Wok* 2F 11
Bridge Clo. *Byfl* 3K 7
Bridge Clo. *Wok* 1E 10
Bridge Ct. *Wok* 1F 11
Bridgehill Clo. *Guild* 2C 22
Bridge Mead. *Pirb* 3F 15
Bridge M. *G'ming* 3A 34
Bridge M. *St J* 1F 11
Bridge Pk. *Guild* 1A 24
Bridge Rd. *G'ming* 2A 34
Bridge St. *G'ming* 3A 34
Bridge St. *Guild* 5E 22 (4B 36)
Bridge St. Pas. *Guild* 4B 36
Brierly Clo. *Guild* 2C 22
Bright Hill. *Guild* 6G 23 (5D 36)
Brighton Rd. *G'ming* 3A 34
Brind Cotts. *Chob* 1B 4
British Red Cross Mus. & Archives. 7A 30
Brittens Clo. *Guild* 6C 16
Broad Acres. *G'ming* 6A 28
Broadacres. *Guild* 2A 22
Broadford. 4F 29
Broadford La. *Chob* 3A 4
Broadford Pk. *Shalf* 4F 29
Broadford Rd. *P'mrsh & Shalf* 5E 28
Broadmead Rd. *Send & Old Wok* 6K 11
Broadmeads. *Wok* 6K 11
Broadoaks Cres. *W Byf* 4F 7
Broad St. *Guild* 2J 21
Broad St. *W End* 4D 2
Broad Street Common. 1K 21
Broadwater Clo. *Wok* 3B 6
Broadwater La. *G'ming* 1B 34
Broadwater Ri. *Guild* 5J 23
Broadway. *Knap* 2H 9
Broadway Ct. *Knap* 1J 9
Broadway Ho. *Knap* 2J 9
Broadway Rd. *Light & W'sham* 1C 2
Broadway, The. *New H* 1E 6
Broadway, The. *Wok* 1H 11
Brockenhurst Clo. *Wok* 5H 5
Brockhill. *Wok* 1C 10
Brocks Clo. *G'ming* 2C 34
Brocks Dri. *Guild* 7J 15
Brockway Clo. *Guild* 3K 23
Brodie Rd. *Guild* 5G 23 (4E 36)
Broke Ct. *Guild* 1A 24
Brook. 5J 31
Brooke Forest. *Guild* 7J 15
Brookfield. *G'ming* 6C 28

38 A-Z Guildford & Woking

Brookfield—Condor Ct.

Brookfield. Wok. 7D 4
Brook Grn. Chob 1B 4
(off Chertsey Rd.)
Brook Hill. Alb. 6H 31
Brooklands. 1K 7
Brooklands Bus. Pk. Wey. 2J 7
Brooklands Ct. New H. 1H 7
Brooklands Rd. Wey 2K 7
Brook La. Alb 5J 31
Brook La. Chob 2K 3
Brook La. Send 6C 12
Brookleys. Chob 1B 4
Brooklyn Clo. Wok 3G 11
Brooklyn Ct. Wok 3G 11
Brooklyn Rd. Wok 2G 11
Brook Mead. Milf. 7F 33
Brook Rd. Chil. 4A 30
Brookside. Guild 6F 17
Brookwell La. Brmly. 6J 35
Brookwood. 4G 9
Brookwood Lye Rd. Brkwd 4H 9
Broomcroft Clo. Wok. 7B 6
Broomcroft Dri. Wok. 6B 6
Broomfield. Guild 3A 22
Broom Fld. Light 3A 2
Broomfield Clo. Guild 2A 22
Broomfield Rd. New H 2F 7
Broomhall End. Wok 7G 5
Broomhall La. Wok 7G 5
Broomhall Rd. Wok. 7G 5
Browell Ho. Guild 3B 24
(off Merrow St.)
Bruce Clo. Byfl 4H 7
Brunswick Dri. Brkwd 4D 8
Brunswick Rd. Brkwd 5A 8
(in two parts)
Brushfield Way. Knap. 3J 9
Bryanstone Av. Guild. 7B 16
Bryanstone Clo. Guild 1B 22
Bryanstone Gro. Guild. 7B 16
Brynford Clo. Wok. 6G 5
Bryony Rd. Guild. 1K 23
Buckingham Clo. Guild 3H 23
Bucks Clo. W Byf. 5F 7
Bullard Cotts. W Cla 2D 24
Bullbeggars La. Wok 7D 4
Bullswater Common. 2G 15
Bullswater Comn. Rd. Pirb 3G 15
Bungalows, The. Guild. 6B 16
Bunyan's La. Knap 5J 3
Bunyard Dri. Wok 5A 6
Burdenshott Hill. Worp 2C 16
Burdenshott Rd. Worp 2C 16
Burden Way. Guild 6D 16
Burdock Clo. Light. 2B 2
Burleigh Gdns. Wok 1H 11
Burlingham Clo. Guild. 2B 24
Burnet Av. Guild 1K 23
Burnet Clo. W End. 4E 2
Burnham Clo. Knap 2K 9
Burnham Ga. Guild 4F 23 (1C 36)
Burnham Rd. Knap 2K 9
Burntcommon. 2D 18
Burntcommon Clo. Rip 2D 18
Burntcommon La. Rip 2E 18
Burnt Pollard La. Light 1E 2
Burpham. 1K 23
Burpham Court Farm. 6H 17
Burpham La. Guild. 6J 17
Burr Hill La. Chob 1B 4
Burrow Hill. 6E 8
Burrows Clo. Guild 3B 22
Burton Dri. Guild. 6G 15
Burwood Clo. Guild. 3B 24
Bury Clo. Wok 7F 5
Bury Fields. Guild 6E 22 (6B 36)
Bury La. Wok. 7E 4
Burys, The. G'ming 2A 34
Bury St. Guild. 6E 22 (6B 36)
Busbridge. 5B 34
Busbridge Lakes Ornamental Wildfowl. 6A 34
Busbridge La. G'ming 4K 33
Busdens Clo. Milf. 7F 33
Busdens La. Milf 7F 33
Busdens Way. Milf. 7F 33
Bush La. Send. 1B 18
Bushy Hill. 3B 24
Bushy Hill Dri. Guild 2K 23
Butt La. P'ham. 1A 26
Butts La. G'ming. 3K 33
(in two parts)
Butts Rd. Wok. 1G 11
Byfleet. 4K 7
Byfleet Ind. Est. Byfl 2H 7
Byfleet Rd. New H. 1H 7
Byfleet Technical Cen. Byfl 2H 7
Bylands. Wok. 3J 11
Byrefield Rd. Guild 1B 22
Byron Clo. Knap 1A 10

C

Cabell Rd. Guild 3K 21
Cadogan Ho. Guild 5H 23
(off St Lukes Sq.)
Caillard Rd. Byfl. 2J 7
Caledon Pl. Guild. 1J 23
Calluna Ct. Wok. 2H 11
Camargue Pl. G'ming 3B 34
Cambridge Clo. Wok 2B 10
Camellia Ct. W End 4F 3
Campbell Av. Wok. 5H 11
Camphill Ct. W Byf 3E 6
Camphill Ind. Est. W Byf 2F 7
Camphill Rd. W Byf. 3E 6
Canada Rd. Byfl. 2H 7
Candlerush Clo. Wok. 1K 11
Canewden Clo. Wok 3G 11
Cannon Cres. Chob 2A 4
Canterbury Rd. Guild. 2B 22
Capital Pk. Wok. 5K 11
Capstans Wharf. St J. 2B 10
Caradon Clo. Wok. 2D 10
Caraway Pl. Guild 6C 16
Cardamom Clo. Guild 7C 16
Cardigan Clo. Wok. 2A 10
Cardingham. Wok 1C 10
Cardwells Keep. Guild. 1C 22
Carlos St. G'ming 3A 34
Carlton Clo. Wok. 5H 5
Carlton Rd. Wok 5J 5
Carmel Clo. Wok 2G 11
Carolyn Clo. Wok. 3B 10
Carroll Av. Guild 4K 23
Cartbridge. 6K 11
Cartbridge Clo. Send 7K 11
Carters Clo. Guild 7G 17
Carters La. Wok. 4A 12
Carthouse Cotts. Guild 1A 24
Carthouse La. Wok 5A 4
Castle Green. 4K 3
Castle Gro. Rd. Chob. 4K 3
Castle Hill. Guild 6F 23 (6C 36)
Castle Rd. Wok 5H 5
Castle Sq. Guild 6F 23 (5D 36)
Castle St. Guild. 6F 23 (5C 36)
Catalpa Clo. Guild 2E 22
Catena Ri. Light. 1A 2
Cater Gdns. Guild 2B 22
Caterham Clo. Pirb 5E 8
Cathedral Clo. Guild 5D 22
Cathedral Ct. Guild 4C 22
Cathedral Hill Ind. Est. Guild 3C 22
Cathedral Precinct. Guild. 5C 22
Cathedral Vw. Guild. 4B 22
Catherine Clo. Byfl. 5J 7
Catteshall. 2C 34
Catteshall Hatch. G'ming. 1C 34
Catteshall La. G'ming 3A 34
Catteshall Rd. G'ming 1C 34
(in two parts)
Catteshall Ter. G'ming 2C 34
(off Catteshall Rd.)
Causeway Ct. Wok. 2B 10
Cavell Way. Knap. 3J 9
Cavendish Rd. Wok 3F 11
Cavenham Clo. Wok 3G 11
Cawsey Way. Wok. 1G 11
Caxton Gdns. Guild. 3D 22
Cedar Gdns. Wok 2D 10
Cedar Gro. Bisl 6G 3
Cedar Ho. Guild. 2A 24
Cedar Rd. Wok 4D 10
Cedars Ct. Guild. 1J 23
Cedars, The. Byfl. 3K 7
Cedars, The. Guild. 1J 23
Cedars, The. Milf 7E 32
Cedars, The. Pirb. 6D 8
Cedar Way. Guild. 2E 22
Celtic Rd. Byfl 5J 7
Cemetery Pales. Brkwd 6F 9
Century Ct. Wok 7H 5
Century Way. Brkwd 3D 8
Chalk La. Shack. 6D 26
Chalk Rd. G'ming 2K 33
Chancellor Ct. Guild. 5K 21
(in two parts)
Channings. Hors 6G 5
Chantry Cotts. Chil 3K 29
Chantry Ind. Pk. Art. 3E 28
Chantry La. Shere 2K 31
Chantry Rd. Chil 3K 29
Chantry Vw. Rd. Guild 7F 23 (7D 36)
Chapel Clo. Milf. 5F 33
Chapel Farm Mobile Home Pk. Norm 1E 20
Chapel Fields. G'ming 7K 27
Chapelhouse Clo. Guild 4A 22
Chapel La. Milf. 5F 33
Chapel La. Pirb 6G 9
Chapel St. Guild 6F 23 (5C 36)
Chapel St. Wok 1H 11
Charlock Way. Guild 1K 23
Charlotte Ct. Guild. 6H 23
Charlotteville. 6H 23
Charterhouse. 7J 27
Charterhouse. G'ming 1H 33
Charterhouse Rd. G'ming 7K 27
CHASE CHILDREN'S HOSPICE. 2E 28
Chasefield Clo. Guild 1J 23
Chase, The. Guild 5C 22
Chatfield Dri. Guild 2A 24
Chatton Row. Bisl 1G 9
Chaucer Ct. Guild 6E 22 (6B 36)
Cheapside. Wok. 5F 5
Cheniston Clo. W Byf. 4E 6
Chequer Tree Clo. Knap. 7A 4
Cherry St. Wok 2G 11
Cherry Tree Av. Guild. 4B 22
Cherry Tree La. G'ming 6K 27
Cherry Tree Rd. Milf 6E 32
Chertsey Rd. Byfl 2H 7
Chertsey Rd. Chob 1B 4
Chertsey Rd. Wok. 1H 11
Chertsey St. Guild. 5F 23 (4D 36)
Cheselden Rd. Guild. 5G 23 (4E 36)
Chesham M. Guild. 5G 23
Chesham Rd. Guild 5H 23
Chester Clo. Guild 2B 22
Chestnut Av. Guild. 7E 22
Chestnut Clo. Rip 2D 18
Chestnut Gro. Wok 4G 11
Chestnut Rd. Guild 4F 23 (1C 36)
Chestnut Wlk. Byfl. 3J 7
Chestnut Way. Brmly. 2J 35
Chestnut Way. G'ming. 5B 34
Chevremont. Guild 5G 23
Cheyne Row. Brmly 7F 35
Chiltern Clo. Wok. 6E 10
Chilworth. 3A 30
Chilworth Hill Cotts. Chil 4C 30
Chilworth Manor. 2B 30
Chilworth Rd. Alb 2E 30
Chinthurst Hill Tower. 6J 29
Chinthurst La. Shalf & Brmly 4G 29
Chinthurst Pk. Shalf 5G 29
Chipstead Ct. Knap 1A 10
Chirton Wlk. Wok 2C 10
Chittenden Cotts. Wis 7J 7
Chittys Common. 7B 16
Chittys Wlk. Guild 7B 16
Chobham. 2A 4
Chobham Pk. Dri. Chob. 1C 4
Chobham Rd. Knap. 2H 9
Chobham Rd. Wok 4E 4
(Station Rd.)
Chobham Rd. Wok 7G 5
(Victoria Way, in two parts)
Choir Grn. Knap. 1A 10
Christchurch Way. Wok. 1H 11
Christie Clo. Guild 1F 23
Christie Clo. Light 1C 2
Christmas Hill. Shalf & Won 4H 29
Christmaspie Av. Norm 4B 20
Church Clo. Brkwd. 5F 9
Church Clo. Guild. 2F 29
Church Clo. Hors 7F 5
Church Clo. Milf. 6F 33
Church End. 5K 13
Churchfields. Guild 6J 17
Churchfields. Hors 7G 5
Church Hill. Hors 7F 5
Church Hill. Pyr. 1D 12
Churchill Rd. Guild 5G 23
Church La. Alb. 2F 31
Church La. Bisl 6G 3
Church La. Pirb. 6D 8
Church La. Send 3K 17
Church La. Worp 4A 16
Church Path. Wok. 1H 11
Church Rd. Byfl 5J 7
Church Rd. Guild 5F 23 (3C 36)
Church Rd. Hors 6G 5
Church Rd. Milf 7F 33
Church Rd. St J. 3C 10
Church Rd. W End. 3F 3
Church St. G'ming. 3K 33
Church St. Old Wok. 5A 12
Church St. E. Wok. 1H 11
Church St. W. Wok 1G 11
Church Wlk. G'ming 1B 34
(in two parts)
Chuters Clo. Byfl 3J 7
Cinder Path. Wok. 3E 10
Cinnamon Gdns. Guild 6C 16
Circle Gdns. Byfl 4K 7
Circle, The. G'ming 1B 34
Circuit Cen., The. Bro I 1J 7
Clandon Ho. Guild 6J 23
Clandon House & Pk. 2E 24
Clandon Park. 2E 24
Clandon Rd. Guild. 5G 23
Clandon Rd. Send 2D 18
Clappers La. Chob 2J 3
Clare Clo. W Byf 4E 6
Claredale. Wok 3G 11
Claremont Av. Wok 3G 11
Claremont Dri. Wok 3G 11
Claremont Rd. W Byf. 3E 6
Claydon Rd. Wok. 7C 4
Clayhanger. Guild 2A 24
Clay La. Guild 5F 17
Clayton Dri. Guild 1B 22
Cleardown. Wok 2K 11
Clearsprings. Light 1A 2
Cleeve, The. Guild 4J 23
Clew's La. Bisl. 7G 3
Cliffe Ri. G'ming 4J 33
Cliffe Rd. G'ming. 5H 33
Clifford Mnr. Rd. Guild 1G 29
Clifton Way. Wok. 1B 10
Cline Rd. Guild 6H 23
Clinton Clo. Knap 2K 9
Clock Ho. Clo. Byfl 3K 7
Clockhouse Ct. Guild. 7E 16
Clockhouse La. Brmly. 1H 35
Clodhouse Hill. Wok 6K 9
Cloisters, The. Wok. 5K 11
Close, The. G'ming 4B 34
Close, The. Light. 1A 2
Close, The. W Byf 4E 6
Close, The. Won 7K 29
Clover Ct. Wok. 2F 11
Clover Lea. G'ming 6A 28
Clover Rd. Guild 3A 22
Club Row. Brkwd 3D 8
Coachlads Av. Guild. 4B 22
Cobbett Hill Rd. Norm. 5E 14
Cobbett Rd. Guild 3B 22
Cobbetts Clo. Norm 6F 15
Cobbetts Clo. Wok 1D 10
Cobbetts Wlk. Bisl. 6G 3
Cobs Way. New H. 1G 7
Codrington Ct. Wok. 2B 10
Colburn Cres. Guild 1J 23
Coldharbour La. W End. 2F 3
Coldharbour La. Wok 6D 6
Coldharbour Rd. W Byf. 5D 6
Coley Av. Wok 2J 11
College Hill. G'ming 5J 33
College La. Wok. 3E 10
College Rd. Guild 5F 23 (3C 36)
College Rd. Wok 7K 5
Collens Fld. Pirb 1F 15
Colliers Clo. Wok. 1D 10
Collier Way. Guild 2B 24
Collingwood Cres. Guild 3J 23
Coltsfoot Dri. Guild 1J 23
Colville Gdns. Light. 2C 2
Colyton Clo. Wok. 2E 10
Combe La. Brmly & Shere 7K 25
Combe La. G'ming & Wmly. 5E 34
Combe Rd. G'ming 6A 28
Comeragh Clo. Wok 4C 10
Commercial Rd. Guild. 5F 23 (4C 36)
Commercial Way. Wok 1G 11
Common Clo. Wok. 5F 5
Commonfields. W End 3G 3
Common La. New H 1G 7
Common, The. 4J 27
Common, The. Shalf. 4G 29
(in two parts)
Common, The. Won 6K 29
Compton.. 3G 27
Compton Ct. Guild 5H 23
Compton Heights. Guild 7K 21
Compton St Nicholas Church. 4G 27
Condor Ct. Guild. 6E 22 (6B 36)

A-Z Guildford & Woking 39

Conford Dri. *Shalf* 4G 29
Coniers Way. *Guild* 1K 23
Conista Ct. *Wok* 7B 4
Coniston Ct. *Light* 1B 2
Coniston Rd. *Wok* 4K 11
Connaught Cres. *Brkwd* 4F 9
Connaught Dri. *Wey* 2K 7
Connaught Rd. *Brkwd* 5E 8
Consort Ct. Wok . . . . 2G 11 *(off York Rd.)*
Constitution Hill. *Wok* 3G 11
Coombe Bottom 7K 25
Coombe La. *Worp* . . . . 6J 15 (in two parts)
Coombes, The. *Brmly* 2J 35
Coombe Way. *Byfl* 3K 7
Cooper Rd. *Guild* 6H 23
Coopers Hill Dri. *Brkwd* 4C 8
Coopers Ri. *G'ming* 4H 33
Copley Clo. *Wok* 3A 10
Copper Beech Clo. *Wok* 5D 10
Coppice Clo. *Guild* 3K 21
Coppice End. *Wok* 7C 6
Copse Clo. *Chil* 4A 30
Copse Rd. *Wok* 2B 10
Copse Side. *G'ming* 6K 27
Copthall Way. *New H* 1D 6
Copthorne Dri. *Light* 1B 2
Coresbrook Way. *Knap* 2G 9
Coriander Cres. *Guild* 6C 16
Corner Bungalows. *G'ming* 6H 27
Corner, The. *W Byf* 4E 6
Cornfields. *G'ming* 6B 28
Cornwall Av. *Byfl* 5K 7
Corrie Rd. *Wok* 4K 11
Cotteslow Clo. *Bisl* 7F 3
Cotts Wood Dri. *Guild* 6J 17
Council Cotts. *W End* 3F 3
Council Cotts. *Wis* 6H 7
Courtenay M. *Wok* 7J 5
Courtenay Rd. *Wok* 7J 5
Court Grn. Heights. *Wok* 4E 10
Court, The. *Guild* 6E 22 (6B 36)
Court Yd., The. *W Byf* 3E 6
Cow La. *G'ming* 3K 33
Cowshot Common 4E 8
Cowshot Cres. *Brkwd* 4D 8
Cowslip La. *Hors* 6D 4
Craigmore Tower. Wok . . . . 3G 11 *(off Guildford Rd.)*
Cranfield Ct. *St J* 2C 10
Cranleigh Rd. *Won* 7K 29
Cranley Clo. *Guild* 4J 23
Cranley Dene. *Guild* 4J 23
Cranley Pl. *Knap* 2K 9
Cranley Rd. *Guild* 4H 23
Cranstoun Clo. *Guild* 7B 16
Crescent, The. *Guild* 3C 22
Cresta Dri. *Wdhm* 1D 6
Creston Av. *Knap* 7A 4
Creswell Corner. *Knap* 1K 9
Crickets Hill 2K 17
Crockery La. *E Clan* 6H 19
Croft Rd. *G'ming* 3K 33
Cromar Ct. *Hors* 7E 4
Crossacres. *Wok* 7C 6
Cross Lanes. *Guild* 4H 23
Crossways, The. *Guild* 6B 22
Crown Ct. *G'ming* 3A 34
Crown Heights. *Guild* 7G 23 (7E 36)
Crownpits 4B 34
Crownpits La. *G'ming* 4A 34
Crown Sq. *Wok* 1H 11
Crown Wlk. *G'ming* 3A 34
Cubitt Way. *Knap* 2K 9
Cuckoo La. *W End* 4D 2
Cuckoo Va. *W End* 4D 2
Cull's Rd. *Norm* 4B 20
Culworth Ho. *Guild* 5G 23
Cumberland Av. *Guild* 6C 16
Cunningham Av. *Guild* 3J 23
Curlew Gdns. *Guild* 2B 24
Curling Va. *Guild* 6C 22
Cygnet Clo. *Wok* 7D 4
Cypress Rd. *Guild* 2E 22

D

Daffodil Dri. *Bisl* 7G 3
Dagden Rd. *Shalf* 3G 29
Dagley Farm Cvn. Pk. *Shalf* 3F 29
Dagley La. *Shalf* 2F 29
Dairyman's Wlk. *Guild* 6K 17
Dale Vw. *Wok* 2D 10
Damask Clo. *W End* 4E 2
Dane Ct. *Wok* 6D 6
Danesfield. *Rip* 7D 12
Danes Hill. *Wok* 2J 11
Danesrood. *Guild* 5H 23
Danone Ct. *Guild* 4F 23 (2C 36)
Danses Clo. *Guild* 2B 24
Dapdune Ct. *Guild* 4E 22 (2B 36)
Dapdune Rd. *Guild* 4F 23 (2C 36)
Dapdune Wharf. 4E 22 (2A 36)
Darfield Rd. *Guild* 1J 23
Dark La. *P'ham* 2B 26
Dark La. *Shere* 2K 31
Dartmouth Av. *Wok* 5A 6
Dartmouth Grn. *Wok* 5B 6
Dartmouth Path. *Wok* 5B 6
Dartnell Av. *W Byf* 3F 7
Dartnell Clo. *W Byf* 3F 7
Dartnell Ct. *W Byf* 3G 7
Dartnell Cres. *W Byf* 3F 7
Dartnell Park 3G 7
Dartnell Pk. Rd. *W Byf* 3F 7
Dartnell Pl. *W Byf* 3F 7
Darvel Clo. *Wok* 7C 4
Daryngton Dri. *Guild* 4K 23
Dashwood Clo. *W Byf* 3G 7
Davies Clo. *G'ming* 7K 27
Davis Rd. *Wey* 1K 7
Davos Clo. *Wok* 3G 11
Dawney Hill. *Pirb* 5E 8
Dawneys Rd. *Pirb* 6E 8
Dawson Rd. *Byfl* 2H 7
Dayspring. *Guild* 7D 16
Deacon Fld. *Guild* 3C 22
Dean Clo. *Wok* 7C 6
Deanery Pl. G'ming . . . . 3K 33 *(off Church St.)*
Deanery Rd. *G'ming* 2K 33
Dean Rd. *G'ming* 1K 33
Dedswell Dri. *W Cla* 6E 18
Deep Pool La. *Hors* 5D 4
Deeprose Clo. *Guild* 7D 16
Deerbarn Rd. *Guild* 3D 22
Deer Leap. *Light* 2A 2
Deers Farm Clo. *Wis* 7J 7
De Havilland Dri. *Wey* 2J 7
De Lara Way. *Wok* 2F 11
Dell, The. *Wok* 3E 10
Delta Clo. *Chob* 1B 4
Delta Rd. *Chob* 1B 4
Delta Rd. *Wok* 7J 5
Denehyrst Ct. Guild . . . . 5G 23 *(off York Rd.)*
Dene Pl. *Wok* 2E 10
Dene Rd. *Guild* 5G 23 (3E 36)
Denholm Gdns. *Guild* 1J 23
Denly Way. *Light* 1C 2
Denmark Rd. *Guild* 5G 23 (3E 36)
Dennisville 5C 22
Dennis Way. *Guild & Sly I* 6G 17
Denton Way. *Wok* 1B 10
Denvale Wlk. *Wok* 2C 10
Denzil Rd. *Guild* 5D 22 (4A 36)
Derby Rd. *Guild* 4B 22
Derrydown. *Wok* 5E 10
Derwent Rd. *Light* 2B 2
Devoil Clo. *Guild* 7K 17
Devon Bank. *Guild* 7E 22 (7B 36)
Devonshire Av. *Wok* 5A 6
Dianthus Ct. *Wok* 2F 11
Digby Way. *Byfl* 3K 7
Dillon Cotts. *Guild* 6A 18
Dinsdale Clo. *Wok* 2J 11
Dixon Dri. *Wey* 1K 7
Dodds Cres. *W Byf* 5F 7
Dodd's La. *Wok* . . . . 5E 6 (in two parts)
Donkey Town 4D 2
Donnafields. *Bisl* 7G 3
Donne Gdns. *Wok* 6C 6
Dorchester Ct. *Wok* 7J 5
Dorincourt. *Wok* 6C 6
Dorking Rd. *Chil* 3C 30
Dorking Vs. *Knap* 1K 9
Dormers Clo. *G'ming* 7K 27
Dorrit Cres. *Guild* 2A 22
Dorset Dri. *Wok* 1K 11
Dorset Way. *Byfl* 1H 7
Dorton Way. *Rip* 5F 13
Douglas Clo. *Guild* 5F 17
Douglas Dri. *G'ming* 2B 34
Dovedale Clo. *Guild* 1J 23
Doverfield Rd. *Guild* 1J 23
Doversmead. *Knap* 7A 4
Downer Mdw. *G'ming* 6A 28
Downing Av. *Guild* 5B 22
Down La. *Comp* 3H 27
Down Rd. *Guild* 4K 23
Downside Orchard. *Wok* 1J 11
Downside Rd. *Guild* 5K 23
Downs Link. *Brmly* 6H 29
Downs Link. *Brmly & Sham G* 2J 35
Downs Link. *Chil* 2B 30
Downs Link. *Shalf* 5G 29
Downs Link. *Won & Chil* 5K 29
Downsview Av. *Wok* 5H 11
Downsview Ct. *Guild* 7E 16
Downsway. *Guild* 4C 24
Drakes Way. *Wok* 6F 11
Dray Ct. *Guild* 5D 22
Drive, The. *G'ming* 5A 34
Drive, The. *Guild* . . . . 4B 22 (Beech Gro.)
Drive, The. *Guild* . . . . 6B 22 (Farnham Rd.)
Drive, The. *Guild* . . . . 1D 28 (Sandy La.)
Drive, The. *Pep H* . . . . 3E 32 (in two parts)
Drive, The. *Wok* 4D 10
Drive, The. *Won* 1K 35
Drodges Clo. *Brmly* 6H 29
Drove Rd. *Alb* 6J 25
Drove Rd. *Guild* . . . . 6D 24 (in two parts)
Drummond Rd. *Guild* 4F 23 (2C 36)
Dukes Ct. *Wok* 1H 11
Duke's Dri. *G'ming* 7H 27
Duke St. *Wok* 1H 11
Duncan Dri. *Guild* 3J 23
Duncombe Rd. *G'ming* 5K 33
Dunfee Way. *W Byf* 3J 7
Dunlin Ri. *Guild* 2B 24
Dunmore. *Guild* 3K 21
Dunmow Ho. *Byfl* 4J 7
Dunnets. *Knap* 1A 10
Dunsborough Park 4G 13
Dunsdon Av. *Guild* 5D 22
Durham Clo. *Guild* 2B 22
Dykes Path. *Wok* 6A 6
Dynevor Pl. *Guild* 7J 15

E

Eagle Rd. *Guild* 4F 23 (2D 36)
Eashing 3F 33
Eashing Bridge. 4E 32
Eashing La. *Milf & G'ming* 5F 33
Easington Pl. *Guild* 5H 23
Eastbrook Clo. *Wok* 7J 5
Eastbury La. *Comp* 3G 27
East Clandon 1H 25
Eastcroft Ct. *Guild* 5J 23
E. Flexford La. *Wanb* 6F 21
East Gdns. *Wok* 1A 12
Eastgate Gdns. *Guild* 5G 23 (3E 36)
East Hill. *Wok* 7A 6
Eastmead. *Wok* 1D 10
East Meads. *Guild* 5B 22
East Shalford 3K 29
E. Shalford La. *Guild* 2G 29
East Way. *Guild* 4B 22
Eastwood Lodge. *Brmly* 7H 29
Eastwood Rd. *Brmly* 7H 29
Eaton Ct. *Guild* 2J 23
Eaton Ho. Guild . . . . 6H 23 *(off St Lukes Sq.)*
Ebbage Ct. *Wok* 2G 11
Echo Pit Rd. *Guild* 1G 29
Ecob Clo. *Guild* 7B 16
Eden Clo. *New H* 1F 7
Edencroft. *Brmly* 7H 29
Eden Gro. Rd. *Byfl* 4J 7
Edgeborough Ct. *Guild* 5H 23
Edge Hill. *Guild* 5H 23
Edgeley Cvn. Pk. *Alb* 6J 31
Edward II Av. *Byfl* 5K 7
Effingham Ct. Wok . . . . 3G 11 *(off Constitution Hill)*
Egerton Ct. *Guild* 4A 22
Egerton Rd. *Guild* 4A 22
Egley Dri. *Wok* 6F 11
Egley Rd. *Wok* . . . . 6F 11 (in two parts)
Elcho Rd. *Brkwd* 3C 8
Elder Clo. *Guild* 1J 23
Elder Rd. *Bisl* 6G 3
Eleanor Ct. *Guild* 6F 23 (5D 36)
Electric Theatre, The. 5E 22 (4B 36)
Elgin Gdns. *Guild* 3J 23
Elizabeth Ct. *G'ming* 7A 28
Elizabeth Rd. *G'ming* 7A 28
Elkins Gdns. *Guild* 1J 23
Elles Av. *Guild* 4A 24
Ellingham. *Wok* 3G 11
Ellis Av. *Onsl* 6B 22
Ellis Farm Clo. *Wok* 6F 11
Elmbank Av. *Guild* 5C 22
Elm Bri. Est. *Wok* 3H 11
Elmbridge La. *Wok* 3H 11
Elm Clo. *Rip* 1E 18
Elm Clo. *Wok* 6F 5
Elm Ct. *Knap* 1K 9
Elm Dri. *Chob* 1B 4
Elm Fld. Cotts. *Wood S* 3G 21
Elmfield Ho. *Guild* 2A 24
Elm Gro. *Bisl* 7G 3
Elmgrove Clo. *Wok* 3K 9
Elm Hill 1A 20
Elmhurst Ct. *Guild* 5H 23
Elm Rd. *G'ming* 6B 28
Elm Rd. *Wok* . . . . 2F 11 (Kingsway)
Elm Rd. *Wok* . . . . 6H 5 (Woodham Ri.)
Elmside. *Guild* 5C 22
Elmside. *Milf* 6F 33
Elmstead Rd. *W Byf* 4E 6
Elmtree Clo. *Byfl* 4J 7
Elmwood Rd. *Wok* 3K 9
Elphinstone Clo. *Brkwd* 5F 9
Elsdon Rd. *Wok* 2C 10
Elstead Rd. *Shack* 1C 32
Elveden Clo. *Wok* 1F 13
Ely Pl. *Guild* 2B 22
Emmanuel Clo. *Guild* 1C 22
Emmetts Clo. *Wok* 1F 11
Englefield Rd. *Knap* 1J 9
Engliff La. *Wok* 7E 6
Ennismore Av. *Guild* 4H 23
Enterprise Est. *Guild* 7G 17
Envis Way. *Guild* 7J 15
Epsom Rd. *E Clan & W Hor* 1J 25
Epsom Rd. *Guild* 5G 23 (4E 36)
Erica Clo. *W End* 4E 2
Erica Ct. *Wok* 2F 11
Escombe Dri. *Guild* 6D 16
Europa Pk. Rd. *Guild* 3E 22
Eustace Rd. *Guild* 2B 24
Evelyn Clo. *Wok* 4F 11
Everest Ct. *Wok* 7A 4
Everlands Clo. *Wok* 2G 11
Eve Rd. *Wok* 6K 5
Exeter Pl. *Guild* 2B 22
Eyston Dri. *Wey* 1K 7

F

Fairborne Way. *Guild* 1C 22
Fairbourne Clo. *Wok* 2C 10
Fairfax Rd. *Wok* 4K 11
Fairfield Clo. *Guild* 3C 22
Fairfield La. *W End* 3G 3
Fairfield Lodge. *Guild* 3C 22
Fairfield Ri. *Guild* 3B 22
Fairford Clo. *W Byf* 5D 6
Fairlands 7J 15
Fairlands Av. *Guild* 7J 15
Fairlands Ct. *Guild* 7J 15
Fairlands Rd. *Guild* 6J 15
Fairlawn Pk. *Wok* 5G 5
Fairlawns. *Guild* 4A 24
Fairlawns. *Wdhm* 2D 6
Fairmead. *Wok* 2E 10
Fairoaks Airport 1G 5
Fairoaks Cvn. Pk. *Guild* 6G 15
Fairview Av. *Wok* 2G 11
Fairview Clo. *Wok* 2H 11
Fairwater Dri. *New H* 1H 7
Fairway. *Guild* 3B 24
Fairway Clo. *Wok* 3D 10
Fairway, The. *G'ming* 5B 34
Fairway, The. *Wey* 2K 7
Fairway, The. *Worp* 1J 15
Falcon Clo. *Light* 2A 2
Falcon Ct. *Wok* 4A 6
Falcon Rd. *Guild* . . . . 5F 23 (3D 36) (in two parts)
Falstone. *Wok* 2D 10
Faris Barn Dri. *Wdhm* 3D 6
Faris La. *Wdhm* 2D 6
Farleigh Ct. *Guild* 4A 22
Farleigh Rd. *New H* 2E 6
Farley Green 6H 31
Farley Heath 7G 31

Farley Heath Rd.—Halley's App.

Farley Heath Rd. *Alb* . . . 7G 31
Farm Clo. *Byfl* . . . 3K 7
Farm Clo. *Guild* . . . 1F 23
Farm Clo. *Worp* . . . 6J 15
Farm Ho. Clo. *Wok* . . . 6B 6
Farm La. *Send* . . . 1A 18
Farm Rd. *Wok* . . . 4K 11
Farm Wlk. *Guild* . . . 6B 22
Farncombe. . . . 7A 28
Farncombe Hill. *G'ming* . . . 7K 27 (in two parts)
Farncombe St. *G'ming* . . . 7A 28
Farnham Rd. *Guild* . . . 7K 21 (5A 36)
FARNHAM ROAD HOSPITAL. . . . 5D 22
Farnley. *Wok* . . . 1B 10
Farriers, The. *Brmly* . . . 2J 35
Farthings. *Knap* . . . 7A 4
Felix Dri. *W Cla* . . . 5E 18
Fellow Grn. *W End* . . . 4F 3
Fellow Grn. Rd. *W End* . . . 4F 3
Fennel Clo. *Guild* . . . 1K 23
Fennscombe Ct. *W End* . . . 4E 2
Fenns La. *W End* . . . 4E 2
Fenns Way. *Wok* . . . 6G 5
Fentum Rd. *Guild* . . . 2C 22
Fenwick Clo. *Wok* . . . 2D 10
Ferndale. *Guild* . . . 2A 22
Ferndale Rd. *Wok* . . . 7H 5
Fernden Ri. *G'ming* . . . 7A 28
Ferndown Clo. *Guild* . . . 5J 23
Ferndown Ct. *Guild* . . . 3E 22
Ferney Ct. *Byfl* . . . 3H 7
Ferney Rd. *Byfl* . . . 3H 7
Fernhill Clo. *Wok* . . . 4E 10
Fernhill La. *Wok* . . . 4E 10 (in two parts)
Fernhill Pk. *Wok* . . . 4E 10
Fernihough Clo. *Wey* . . . 1K 7
Fernley Ho. *G'ming* . . . 6A 28
Fern Rd. *G'ming* . . . 1B 34
Ferry La. *Guild* . . . 1E 28
Field Clo. *Guild* . . . 2B 24
Field End. *W End* . . . 4F 3
Fielders Grn. *Guild* . . . 4J 23
Fieldings, The. *Wok* . . . 7B 4
Field La. *G'ming* . . . 7B 28
Field Pl. *G'ming* . . . 7A 28
Fld. View Cotts. *G'ming* . . . 3H 33
Field Way. *Rip* . . . 2D 18
Filmer Gro. *G'ming* . . . 2A 34
Finch Clo. *Knap* . . . 1J 9
Finches Ri. *Guild* . . . 2K 23
Finch Rd. *Guild* . . . 4F 23 (2D 36)
Findlay Dri. *Guild* . . . 7B 16
Firbank Dri. *Wok* . . . 3D 10
Firbank La. *Wok* . . . 3D 10
Fircroft Clo. *Wok* . . . 2H 11
Fircroft Ct. *Wok* . . . 2H 11
Firgrove. *Wok* . . . 3D 10
Firs Av. *Brmly* . . . 1J 35
Firs, The. *Bisl* . . . 7G 3
Firs, The. *Byfl* . . . 3H 7
Firs, The. *Guild* . . . 1D 28
Firsway. *Guild* . . . 3B 22
Fir Tree Rd. *Guild* . . . 1E 22
Firwood Clo. *Wok* . . . 3A 10
Fisher Rowe Clo. *Brmly* . . . 1J 35
Fitzjohn Clo. *Guild* . . . 1A 24
Five Oaks Clo. *Wok* . . . 3K 9
Flambard Way. *G'ming* . . . 3K 33
Fleetwood Ct. *W Byf* . . . 4E 6
Flexford. . . . 4B 20
Flexford Rd. *Norm* . . . 5B 20 (in two parts)
Flexlands La. *W End* . . . 1H 3
Flitwick Grange. *Milf* . . . 6F 33
Florence Av. *New H* . . . 2E 6
Florence Ct. *Knap* . . . 2J 9
Florence Way. *Knap* . . . 2J 9
Florida Rd. *Shalf* . . . 3G 29
Flower Wlk. *Guild* . . . 7E 22 (7B 36)
Floyd's La. *Wok* . . . 7E 6
Folly, The. *Light* . . . 3B 2
Forbench Clo. *Rip* . . . 6F 13
Ford Rd. *Bisl* . . . 5E 2
Ford Rd. *Chob* . . . 1J 3
Ford Rd. *Wok* . . . 4K 11
Forest Clo. *Wok* . . . 6B 6
Foresters Clo. *Wok* . . . 2B 10
Forest Rd. *Wok* . . . 6B 6
Forge End. *Wok* . . . 1G 11
Forsythia Pl. *Guild* . . . 2E 22
Forsyth Path. *Wok* . . . 4B 6
Forsyth Rd. *Wok* . . . 5A 6
Fort Rd. *Guild* . . . 7G 23 (7E 36)
Fosse Way. *W Byf* . . . 4D 6
Fosters La. *Knap* . . . 1J 9
Four Acres. *Guild* . . . 2A 24
Fowlerscroft. *Comp* . . . 4H 27
Fowlers Mead. *Chob* . . . 1A 4
Foxborough Hill. *Brmly* . . . 7F 29
Foxborough Hill Rd. *Brmly* . . . 7F 29
Foxburrows Av. *Guild* . . . 4B 22
Foxburrows Ct. *Guild* . . . 3B 22
Fox Clo. *Wok* . . . 6B 6
Fox Corner. . . . 2J 15
Fox Covert. *Light* . . . 2A 2
Fox Dene. *G'ming* . . . 5J 33
Foxenden Rd. *Guild* . . . 5G 23 (3E 36)
Foxes Path. *Sut G* . . . 3H 17
Foxglove Gdns. *Guild* . . . 2A 24
Foxgrove Dri. *Wok* . . . 6J 5
Foxhanger Gdns. *Wok* . . . 7J 5
Fox Hills. *Wok* . . . 1E 10
Foxlake Rd. *Byfl* . . . 3K 7
Frailey Clo. *Wok* . . . 7K 5
Frailey Hill. *Wok* . . . 7K 5
Francis Ct. *Guild* . . . 2D 22
Franklin Ct. Guild . . . *4B 22* *(off Derby Rd.)*
Franklyn Rd. *G'ming* . . . 4H 33
Franks Rd. *Guild* . . . 1C 22
Frederick Sanger Rd. *Sur R* . . . 5K 21
Freesia Dri. *Bisl* . . . 7G 3
French's Wells. *Wok* . . . 1D 10
Freshborough Ct. *Guild* . . . 5H 23
Friar's Ga. *Guild* . . . 6C 22
Friars Ri. *Wok* . . . 2J 11
Friary Bri. *Guild* . . . 6E 22 (5B 36)
Friary Ct. *Wok* . . . 2B 10
Friary Pas. *Guild* . . . 6E 22 (5B 36)
Friary St. *Guild* . . . 6F 23 (5B 36)
Friary, The. *Guild* . . . 5E 22 (4B 36)
Frith Hill. . . . 1K 33
Frith Hill Rd. *G'ming* . . . 7K 27
Frobisher Gdns. *Guild* . . . 3J 23
Frog Gro. La. *Wood S* . . . 2F 21
Frog La. *Sut G* . . . 2G 17
Fuchsia Way. *W End* . . . 4E 2
Fulbrook Av. *New H* . . . 2E 6
Fullerton Clo. *Byfl* . . . 5K 7
Fullerton Dri. *Byfl* . . . 5J 7
Fullerton Rd. *Byfl* . . . 5J 7
Fullerton Way. *Byfl* . . . 5J 7
Fullmer Way. *Wdhm* . . . 1D 6
Furlough, The. *Wok* . . . 7J 5
Furzehill Cotts. *Pirb* . . . 6C 8
Furze La. *G'ming* . . . 6B 28

G

Gables Clo. *Kingf* . . . 4H 11 (in two parts)
Gables Ct. *Kingf* . . . 4H 11
Gale Dri. *Light* . . . 1A 2
Gales Clo. *Guild* . . . 1B 24
Gallery Rd. *Brkwd* . . . 3D 8
Galvins Clo. *Guild* . . . 1C 22
Gambles La. *Rip* . . . 1G 19
Ganghill. *Guild* . . . 2J 23
Gapemouth Rd. *Pirb* . . . 6A 8
Gardenia Dri. *W End* . . . 4F 3
Gardens, The. *Pirb* . . . 6F 9
Gardner Rd. *Guild* . . . 4F 23 (1C 36)
Gate St. *Brmly* . . . 6J 35 (in two parts)
Gateways. *Guild* . . . 4J 23
Gateway, The. *Wok* . . . 5K 5
Gatley Dri. *Guild* . . . 1H 23
Gatwick. . . . 1A 32
Gaveston Clo. *Byfl* . . . 4K 7
Genesis Bus. Pk. *Wok* . . . 6A 6
Genyn Rd. *Guild* . . . 5D 22 (4A 36)
Georgelands. *Rip* . . . 5F 13
George Rd. *G'ming* . . . 7A 28
George Rd. *Guild* . . . 4F 23 (2C 36)
George Rd. *Milf* . . . 5F 33
George St. *Brkwd* . . . 5A 8
Germander Dri. *Bisl* . . . 6G 3
Gibb's Acre. *Pirb* . . . 7F 9
Giffard Way. *Guild* . . . 1C 22
Gill Av. *Guild* . . . 5A 22
Gilliat Dri. *Guild* . . . 2B 24
Glade, The. *W Byf* . . . 4C 6
Glaziers La. *Norm* . . . 2B 20
Glebe Clo. *Light* . . . 1C 2
Glebe Cotts. *W Cla* . . . 2F 25
Glebe Ct. *Guild* . . . 4H 23
Glebe Gdns. *Byfl* . . . 5H 7
Glen Ct. *St J* . . . 3C 10
Glendale Clo. *Wok* . . . 2E 10
Glendale Dri. *Guild* . . . 1A 24
Gloster Rd. *Wok* . . . 4J 11
Gloucester Rd. *Guild* . . . 2B 22
Gloucester Sq. *Wok* . . . 1G 11
Gloucester Wlk. *Wok* . . . 1G 11
Godalming. . . . 3A 34
Godalming Bus. Cen. *G'ming* . . . 3B 34
Godalming Mus. . . . 3K 33
Godley Rd. *Byfl* . . . 5K 7
Goldfinch Gdns. *Guild* . . . 3B 24
Goldfort Wlk. *Wok* . . . 7A 4
Goldings, The. *Wok* . . . 7B 4
Goldsmiths Clo. *Wok* . . . 2E 10
Goldsworth. . . . 2F 11
Goldsworth Orchard. *Wok* . . . 2C 10
Goldsworth Park. . . . 1C 10
Goldsworth Pk. Cen., The. *Wok* . . . 1C 10
Goldsworth Pk. Trad. Est. *Wok* . . . 7D 4
Goldsworth Rd. *Wok* . . . 2E 10
Gole Rd. *Pirb* . . . 5C 8
Golf Clo. *Wok* . . . 5C 6
Golf Club Rd. *Wok* . . . 4C 10
Goose La. *Wok* . . . 6D 10
Goose Rye Rd. *Worp* . . . 3K 15
Gorse Bank. *Light* . . . 3A 2
Gorse Ct. *Guild* . . . 2A 24
Gorselands Clo. *W Byf* . . . 2G 7
Gorsewood Rd. *Wok* . . . 3K 9
Gosden Clo. *Brmly* . . . 6H 29
Gosden Common. . . . 6G 29
Gosden Comn. *Brmly* . . . 7G 29
Gosden Cotts. *Brmly* . . . 7H 29
Gosden Hill Rd. *Guild* . . . 7A 18
Gosden Rd. *W End* . . . 4F 3
Gould Ct. *Guild* . . . 2B 24
Grafham. . . . 7K 35
Grafton Clo. *W Byf* . . . 4D 6
Grandis Cotts. *Rip* . . . 6F 13
Grange Clo. *G'ming* . . . 2C 34
Grange Clo. *Guild* . . . 7D 16
Grange Dri. *Wok* . . . 6G 5
Grangefields Rd. *Guild* . . . 5F 17
Grange Pk. *Wok* . . . 6G 5
Grange Rd. *Guild* . . . 6D 16
Grange Rd. *New H* . . . 1E 6
Grange Rd. *Pirb* . . . 6C 8
Grange Rd. *Wok* . . . 5G 5
Grange, The. *Chob* . . . 1A 4
Grantley Av. *Won* . . . 1K 35
Grantley Clo. *Shalf* . . . 4G 29
Grantley Gdns. *Guild* . . . 3C 22
Grantley Rd. *Guild* . . . 3C 22
Granville Clo. *Byfl* . . . 4K 7
Granville Rd. *Wok* . . . 4H 11
Grasmere Clo. *Guild* . . . 3K 23
Grasmere Rd. *Light* . . . 1B 2
Grasmere Way. *Byfl* . . . 3K 7
Gravetts La. *Guild* . . . 7A 16
Graylands. *Wok* . . . 7G 5
Graylands Clo. *Wok* . . . 7G 5
Graylands Ct. *Guild* . . . 5H 23
Grays Rd. *G'ming* . . . 7B 28
Greatford Dri. *Guild* . . . 4B 24
Gt. George St. *G'ming* . . . 3A 34
Gt. Goodwin Dri. *Guild* . . . 2K 23
Gt. Oaks Pk. *Guild* . . . 6K 17
Great Quarry. *Guild* . . . 7F 23 (7D 36)
Green Acre. *Knap* . . . 7A 4
Greencroft. *Guild* . . . 4K 23
Green Dri. *Rip* . . . 7D 12
Greenham Wlk. *Wok* . . . 2E 10
Greenheys Pl. *Wok* . . . 2H 11
Greenhill Clo. *G'ming* . . . 4K 33
Greenhill Gdns. *Guild* . . . 2A 24
Green La. *Byfl* . . . 3K 7
Green La. *Chob* . . . 1B 4
Green La. *G'ming* . . . 5K 27
Green La. *Guild* . . . 4K 23
Green La. *Milf* . . . 7E 32
Green La. *Sham G* . . . 7E 30
Green La. *W Cla* . . . 4E 18
Green La. *Wok* . . . 5D 10
Green La. *Wood S* . . . 2G 21
Green La. Clo. *Byfl* . . . 3K 7
Green La. E. *Norm* . . . 5A 20 (in two parts)
Greenmeads. *Wok* . . . 6G 11
Greenside Clo. *Guild* . . . 2A 24
Greenside Cotts. *Rip* . . . 5G 13
Green, The. . . . 7F 9
Green, The. *Rip* . . . 5G 13
Greenvale Rd. *Knap* . . . 2K 9
Greenway Clo. *W Byf* . . . 4E 6
Greenwood Clo. *Wdhm* . . . 2D 6
Greenwood Rd. *Brkwd* . . . 5B 8
Greenwood Rd. *Wok* . . . 4A 10
Greenwood, The. *Guild* . . . 3J 23
Gregory Clo. *Wok* . . . 1E 10
Grenville Rd. *Shack* . . . 7D 26
Greville Clo. *Guild* . . . 4A 22
Greyfriars Dri. *Bisl* . . . 6G 3
Greyfriars Rd. *Rip* . . . 1E 18
Greythorne Rd. *Wok* . . . 2C 10
Greywaters. *Brmly* . . . 1J 35
Grindstone Cres. *Knap* . . . 2H 9
Grindstone Handle Corner. . . . 2H 9
Grobars Av. *Wok* . . . 6E 4
Groom Wlk. *Guild* . . . 1G 23
Grosvenor Ct. *Guild* . . . 1K 23
Grosvenor Ho. *Guild* . . . 5H 23
Grosvenor Pl. Wok . . . *1H 11* *(off Burleigh Gdns.)*
Grosvenor Rd. *Chob* . . . 4K 3
Grosvenor Rd. *G'ming* . . . 4A 34
Grove Heath. . . . 7F 13
Gro. Heath Ct. *Rip* . . . 1G 19
Gro. Heath N. *Rip* . . . 6F 13
Gro. Heath Rd. *Rip* . . . 7F 13
Grove Rd. *G'ming* . . . 4J 33
Grove Rd. *Guild* . . . 4A 24
Grove Rd. *Wok* . . . 7H 5
Grovers Farm Cotts. *Wdhm* . . . 2C 6
Grove, The. *Wok* . . . 7H 5
Guernsey Clo. *Guild* . . . 6J 17
Guernsey Farm Dri. *Wok* . . . 6F 5
Guildcroft. *Guild* . . . 4J 23
Guildford. . . . 4C 22 (5C 36)
Guildford & Godalming By-Pass Rd. *Guild* . . . 3G 27
Guildford & Godalming By-Pass Rd. *Milf & Comp* . . . 6E 32
Guildford & Godalming By-Pass Rd. *Shack & Comp* . . . 3E 32
Guildford Bus. Pk. *Guild* . . . 3D 22
Guildford Bus. Pk. Rd. *Guild* . . . 3D 22
Guildford Castle. . . . 6F 23 (5C 36)
Guildford Cathedral. . . . 4D 22
Guildford Ct. *Guild* . . . 4C 22
Guildford Crematorium. *G'ming* . . . 6D 28
Guildford Discovery Cen . . . *5F 23 (4C 36)* *(off Ward St.)*
Guildford Guildhall. . . . *5F 23 (4D 36)* *(off High St.)*
Guildford House Gallery. . . . 5F 23 (4D 36)
Guildford Ind. Est. *Guild* . . . 4C 22
Guildford La. *Alb* . . . 7C 24
Guildford La. *Wok* . . . 3F 11
Guildford Mus. & Art Gallery. . . . 6F 23 (5C 36)
GUILDFORD NUFFIELD HOSPITAL, THE. . . . 4K 21
Guildford Park. . . . 5D 22
Guildford Pk. Av. *Guild* . . . 5D 22 (3A 36)
Guildford Pk. Rd. *Guild* . . . 5D 22 (4A 36)
Guildford Rd. *Cher & Ott* . . . 2K 5
Guildford Rd. *Chob* . . . 5K 3
Guildford Rd. *G'ming* . . . 7C 28
Guildford Rd. *Light & W End* . . . 1A 2
Guildford Rd. *Norm* . . . 1A 20
Guildford Rd. *Pirb* . . . 7F 9
Guildford Rd. *Wok* . . . 6F 11 (Smart's Heath Rd.)
Guildford Rd. *Wok* . . . 3G 11 (Wych Hill La.)
Guildown Av. *Guild* . . . 7D 22 (7A 36)
Guildown Rd. *Guild* . . . 7D 22 (7B 36)
Guileshill La. *Ock* . . . 7J 13
Guinness Ct. *Wok* . . . 2B 10
Gumbrells Clo. *Guild* . . . 7J 15
Gwynne Vaughan Av. *Guild* . . . 7D 16

H

Hacketts La. *Wok* . . . 5D 6
Halebourne La. *Chob & W End* . . . 1G 3
Hale Ends. *Wok* . . . 5D 10
Half Moon Cotts. *Rip* . . . 5G 13
Halfpenny Clo. *Chil* . . . 3B 30
Halfpenny La. *Guild* . . . 7A 24
Halfway La. *G'ming* . . . 3G 33
Hallam Rd. *G'ming* . . . 1B 34
Hall Clo. *G'ming* . . . 7A 28
Hall Dene Clo. *Guild* . . . 3A 24
Halley's App. *Wok* . . . 1C 10

A-Z Guildford & Woking 41

Q

R

Royal Surrey Regiment Mus.—Surrey Ct.

Royal Surrey Regiment Mus. 2E 24
Royston Av. *Byfl* 3J 7
Royston Rd. *Byfl* 3J 7
Rubus Clo. *W End* 4E 2
Rugosa Rd. *W End* 4E 2
Runtley Wood La. *Sut G* 2H 17
Rupert Rd. *Guild* 5E 22 (4A 36)
Ruscoe Dri. *Wok* 1J 11
Rushcroft. *G'ming* 6C 28
Rushett Common. 6K 35
Rushmoor Clo. *Guild* 1B 22
Russell Clo. *Wok* 6E 4
Russell Ct. *Guild* 1E 22
Russell Rd. *Wok* 6E 4
Russetts Clo. *Wok* 6H 5
Rutson Rd. *Byfl* 5K 7
Rydal Pl. *Light* 2B 2
Ryde Clo. *Rip* 5G 13
Ryde Heron. *Knap* 1A 10
Rydens Way. *Wok* 4J 11
Rydes Av. *Guild* 1B 22
Rydes Clo. *Wok* 4A 12
Rydeshill. 2A 22
Ryde's Hill Cres. *Guild* 7B 16
Ryde's Hill Rd. *Guild* 2B 22
Rye Clo. *Guild* 2A 22
Rye Gro. *Light* 1F 3

S

Saddlers Clo. *Guild* 3B 24
Saffron Platt. *Guild* 7C 16
St Albans Clo. *Wood S* 3H 21
St Andrews Clo. *Wok* 1E 10
St Andrew's Ga. *Wok* 2H 11
St Anne's Rd. *G'ming* 2C 34
St Bartholomews Ct. *Guild* 6H 23
St Catherines. *Wok* 3E 10
St Catherine's Ct. *Brmly* 7H 29
St Catherine's Dri. *Guild* 1D 28
St Catherine's Hill. *Guild* 1E 28
St Catherines Pk. *Guild* 6H 23
St Denys Clo. *Knap* 2J 9
St Edmund's Steps. *G'ming* 3K 33
St Hilda's Clo. *Knap* 1K 9
St James Clo. *Wok* 2C 10
St Johns. 3C 10
St John's Clo. *Guild* 5C 22
St John's Ct. *Brkwd* 4F 9
St Johns Ct. *Wok* 3C 10
St John's Hill Rd. *Wok* 3C 10
St John's Lye. *Wok* 3B 10
(in three parts)
St John's M. *Wok* 3C 10
St John's Ri. *Wok* 2D 10
St John's Rd. *Guild* 5B 22
St John's Rd. *Wok* 3B 10
St John's St. *G'ming* 1B 34
St Lawrence Ct. *Chob* 2A 4
St Lawrence Ho. Chob *2A 4*
(off Bagshot Rd.)
St Lukes Ct. *Wok* 5A 6
St Lukes Sq. *Guild* 5H 23
St Margaret's. *Guild* 4H 23
St Martha's Av. *Wok* 5H 11
St Marthas Ct. *Chil* 3K 29
St Martins M. *Pyr* 7E 6
St Marys Garden. *Worp* 4A 16
St Mary's Rd. *Wok* 1E 10
St Marys Way. *Guild* 2A 22
St Michael's Av. *Guild* 6J 15
St Michael's Rd. *Wok* 5B 6
St Mildred's Rd. *Guild* 3H 23
St Nicholas Cres. *Pyr* 7E 6
St Omer Ridge. *Guild* 5J 23
St Omer Rd. *Guild* 5J 23
St Paul's Rd. *Wok* 1J 11
St Peter's Clo. *Wok* 4A 12
St Peter's Rd. *Wok* 5K 11
St Saviours Pl. *Guild* 4E 22 (2B 36)
St Thomas Clo. *Wok* 1E 10
St Thomas Dri. *E Clan* 1J 25
St Thomas's M. *Guild* 6H 23
Salisbury Pl. *W Byf* 2G 7
Salisbury Rd. *Wok* 3G 11
Salt Box Rd. *Worp & Guild* 6B 16
Salvia Ct. *Bisl* 7G 3
Sampleoak La. *Chil* 3C 30
Sandalwood. *Guild* 5D 22
Sandfields. *Send* 1B 18
Sandfield Ter. *Guild* 5F 23 (3C 36)
Sandpit Cotts. *Pirb* 6E 8
Sandpit Hall Rd. *Chob* 3C 4
Sandpit Heath. *Guild* 7K 15
Sandpit La. *Knap* 5H 3
(in two parts)
Sandringham Clo. *Wok* 7E 6
Sandy Clo. *Wok* 1A 12
Sandy La. *Alb* 4G 31
Sandy La. *Comp* 2K 27
Sandy La. *G'ming* 1K 33
Sandy La. *Guild* 2C 28
Sandy La. *Milf* 7E 32
Sandy La. *Norm* 1E 20
Sandy La. *Pyr & Wok* 1E 12
(in two parts)
Sandy La. *Send* 7A 12
Sandy La. *Wok* 1K 11
Sandy Way. *Wok* 1A 12
Sanger Dri. *Send* 7A 12
Sanway. 5J 7
Sanway Clo. *Byfl* 5J 7
Sanway Rd. *Byfl* 5J 7
Sappho Ct. *Wok* 7A 4
Saunders Copse. *Wok* 6D 10
Saunders La. *Wok* 6A 10
Sawpit La. *E Clan* 1J 25
Scarlett Clo. *Wok* 2B 10
Scholars Wlk. *Guild* 5D 22
School Clo. *Bisl* 6F 3
School Clo. *Guild* 1F 23
School Cotts. *Wok* 6E 10
School La. *E Clan* 1J 25
School La. *Norm* 1A 20
School La. *Pirb* 6E 8
School La. *P'ham* 2C 26
School La. *Shack* 1E 32
School La. *Worp* 5A 16
Scillonian Rd. *Guild* 5C 22
Scizdons Climb. *G'ming* 3B 34
Scotland Bri. *New H* 2E 6
Scotland Bri. Rd. *New H* 2E 6
Scott Clo. *Guild* 2C 22
Scott's Gro. Clo. *Chob* 4K 3
Scott's Gro. Rd. *Chob* 4H 3
Scutley La. *Light & W'sham* 1E 2
Scylla Pl. *St J* 3C 10
Seale La. *Seale & P'ham* 2A 26
Sefton Clo. *W End* 4F 3
Selbourne Av. *New H* 1F 7
Selbourne Clo. *New H* 1F 7
Selbourne Rd. *Guild* 1J 23
Selby Wlk. *Wok* 2D 10
Selhurst Clo. *Wok* 6H 5
Sellar's Hill. *G'ming* 7K 27
Sells, The. *Guild* 6H 23
Selsdon Rd. *New H* 2E 6
Selwood Rd. *Wok* 4K 11
Semaphore Rd. *Guild* 6G 23 (6E 36)
Semper Clo. *Knap* 1A 10
Send. 1B 18
Send Barns La. *Send* 1B 18
Send Clo. *Send* 7A 12
Send Hill. *Send* 2A 18
Send Marsh. 7D 12
Send Marsh Grn. *Rip* 7D 12
Send Marsh Rd. *Send* 1B 18
Send Pde. Clo. *Send* 7A 12
Send Rd. *Send* 7K 11
Seymour Rd. *G'ming* 4H 33
Shackleford. 7D 26
Shackleford Rd. *Elst & Shack* 3A 32
Shackleford Rd. *Shack* 7D 26
Shackleford Rd. *Wok* 4J 11
Shackleton Wlk. Guild *4A 22*
(off Chapelhouse Clo.)
Shackstead La. *G'ming* 4J 33
Shadyhanger. *G'ming* 1A 34
Shaftesbury Rd. *Bisl* 7F 3
Shaftesbury Rd. *Wok* 1K 11
Shalford. 3G 29
Shalford Mill. 2G 29
(Disused)
Shalford Rd. *Guild & Shalf* 7F 23 (7D 36)
Shambles, The. *Guild* 6F 23 (5C 36)
Shamrock Cotts. *Guild* 5D 16
Shaws Cotts. Guild *6B 16*
(off Worplesdon Rd.)
Sheepfold Rd. *Guild* 1B 22
Sheeplands Av. *Guild* 2A 24
Sheep Wlk., The. *Wok* 2B 12
Sheerwater. 5B 6
Sheerwater Av. *Wdhm* 3C 6
Sheerwater Rd. *Wok & W Byf* 3C 6
Sheet's Heath La. *Brkwd* 3G 9
Sheldon Ct. *Guild* 5H 23
Shelton Clo. *Guild* 6C 16
Shepherd's Hill. *Guild* 2C 22
Shepherd's La. *Guild* 1B 22
Shepherd's Way. *Guild* 1G 29
(in two parts)
Sherborne Ct. *Guild* 6E 22 (5B 36)
Sherbourne. *Alb* 2H 31
Sherbourne Cotts. *Alb* 1J 31
Shere. 2K 31
Shere Rd. *W Cla & Shere* 5E 24
Sherwood Rd. *Knap* 1A 10
Shetland Clo. *Guild* 6K 17
Shey Copse. *Wok* 1A 12
Shilburn Way. *Wok* 2C 10
Shimmings, The. *Guild* 3J 23
Shires Ho. *Byfl* 4J 7
Shirley Pl. *Knap* 1J 9
Shophouse La. *Alb* 7H 31
Shops, The. *Won* 6K 29
Shores Rd. *Wok* 5G 5
Shrubbs Hill. *Chob* 1J 3
Shrublands Dri. *Light* 2B 2
Silent Pool. 7H 25
Silistria Clo. *Knap* 2J 9
Silo Clo. *G'ming* 6B 28
Silo Dri. *G'ming* 6B 28
Silo Rd. *G'ming* 6B 28
Silver Birch Clo. *Wdhm* 3C 6
Silversmiths Way. *Wok* 2E 10
Silverwood Cotts. *Shere* 1J 31
Simmond's Cotts. *G'ming* 3H 33
Slade Rd. *Brkwd* 4D 8
Slapleys. *Wok* 4G 11
Slocock Hill. *St J* 1E 10
Slyfield Ct. *Guild* 1G 23
Slyfield Green. 1F 23
Slyfield Grn. *Guild* 7G 17
Slyfield Ind. Est. *Sly I* 7G 17
Smart's Heath La. *Wok* 7C 10
Smart's Heath Rd. *Wok* 7B 10
Smith Ct. *Sheer* 4B 6
Snelgate Cotts. *E Clan* 1H 25
Snowdenham La. *Brmly* 2G 35
Snowdenham Links Rd. *Brmly* 1F 35
Snowdrop Way. *Bisl* 1G 9
Sol-y-Vista. *G'ming* 1K 33
Somerswey. *Shalf* 5G 29
Somertons Clo. *Guild* 1C 22
Sopwith Dri. *Bro P & Wey* 2J 7
Sorrel Dri. *Light* 3A 2
South Clo. *Wok* 7E 4
Southcote. *Wok* 6F 5
South Dri. *Brkwd* 5C 8
Southern Bungalows. *Chil* 4K 29
S. Farm La. *Light* 1A 2
South Hill. *G'ming* 3A 34
South Hill. *Guild* 6F 23 (5D 36)
South Rd. *Bisl* 7F 3
South Rd. *Guild* 2D 22
South Rd. *Wok* 6E 4
South St. *G'ming* 3K 33
(in two parts)
S. View Ct. *Wok* 2G 11
Southway. *Guild* 4A 22
Southway Ct. *Guild* 4A 22
Southwood Av. *Knap* 2K 9
Soyer Ct. *Wok* 2A 10
Sparvell Rd. *Knap* 3H 9
Speedwell Clo. *Guild* 1A 24
Spence Av. *Byfl* 5J 7
Spencer Clo. *Wok* 4A 6
Spiceall. *Comp* 4H 27
Spinney, The. *Send* 4G 19
Spring Clo. *G'ming* 6A 28
Spring Ct. *Guild* 7D 16
Springfield. *Light* 2D 2
Springfield Clo. *Knap* 2A 10
Springfield Rd. *Guild* 5G 23 (3E 36)
Springflower Cotts. *Guild* 1J 21
Spring Gro. *G'ming* 6A 28
Springhaven Clo. *Guild* 4J 23
Springside Ct. *Guild* 3E 22
Springwood. *Milf* 6G 33
Sprint Ind. Est. *Byfl* 2H 7
Spruce Dri. *Light* 3A 2
Spur, The. *Knap* 2H 9
Square, The. *Guild* 6B 22
Square, The. *Light* 1C 2
Square, The. *Wis* 7J 7
Squirrel's Clo. *G'ming* 5K 27
Squirrel Wood. *W Byf* 3F 7
Stable Cotts. *G'ming* 7C 28
Stables, The. *Guild* 1F 23
Staffordlake. 2F 9
Stafford Lake. *Knap* 2F 9
Stag Hill. *Guild* 5C 22
Stainton Wlk. *Wok* 2E 10
Stakescorner Rd. *Guild* 5C 28
Stamford Ho. Chob *2A 4*
(off Bagshot Rd.)
Stanford Common. 3E 14
Stanford Cotts. *Pirb* 3E 14
Staniland Dri. *Wey* 2K 7
Stanley Hill. *Pirb* 6C 8
Stanley Rd. *Wok* 7H 5
Stantons Wharf. *Brmly* 7J 29
Staple La. *E Clan & Alb* 2H 25
Star Hill. *Wok* 3E 10
Starwood Clo. *W Byf* 2G 7
Station App. *G'ming* 3K 33
Station App. *Guild* 5G 23 (3E 36)
Station App. *Shalf* 3G 29
Station App. *Wanb* 4B 20
Station App. *W Byf* 3E 6
Station App. *Wok* 2H 11
Station La. *Milf* 6G 33
Station Pl. *G'ming* 7B 28
Station Rd. *Brmly* 1H 35
Station Rd. *Chob* 2B 4
Station Rd. *Farnc* 7B 28
Station Rd. *G'ming* 3K 33
Station Rd. *Shalf* 3G 29
Station Rd. *W Byf* 3E 6
Station Row. *Shalf* 3G 29
Station Vw. *Guild* 5E 22 (3A 36)
Staveley Way. *Knap* 1A 10
Stepbridge Path. *Wok* 1F 11
Stewart Clo. *Wok* 1B 10
Stile Ho. Guild *3B 24*
(off Merrow St.)
Stirling Rd. *Sur R* 4K 21
Stockers La. *Wok* 4H 11
(in two parts)
Stocton Clo. *Guild* 3E 22 (1B 36)
Stocton Rd. *Guild* 3F 23 (1B 36)
Stoke Fields. *Guild* 4F 23 (3C 36)
Stoke Gro. *Guild* 4F 23 (2D 36)
Stoke Hospital. *Guild* 2D 36
Stoke M. *Guild* 5F 23 (3D 36)
Stoke Pk. *Guild* 4F 23 (2D 36)
Stoke Rd. *Guild* 3F 23 (1D 36)
Stonebridge Fields. *Shalf* 4F 29
Stonebridge Wharf. *Shalf* 4F 29
Stonecrop Rd. *Guild* 2A 24
Stonehill Rd. *Chob & Ott* 1E 4
Stonehill Rd. *Light* 1A 2
Stonepit Clo. *G'ming* 3H 33
Stoney Brook. *Guild* 3A 22
Stoop Ct. *W Byf* 3F 7
Storr's La. *Worp* 1J 15
Stoughton. 2C 22
Stoughton Rd. *Guild* 1C 22
Strathcona Gdns. *Knap* 2K 9
(in two parts)
Stratton Ct. *Guild* 2C 22
Strawberry Clo. *Brkwd* 5D 8
Strawberry Fields. *Bisl* 6G 3
Strawberry Ri. *Bisl* 6G 3
Stream Clo. *Byfl* 3H 7
Streeters Clo. *G'ming* 1C 34
Streets Heath. *W End* 3F 3
(in two parts)
Street, The. *Alb* 2F 31
Street, The. *Comp* 3G 27
Street, The. *E Clan* 1H 25
Street, The. *P'ham* 2B 26
Street, The. *Shack* 6C 26
Street, The. *Shalf* 2F 29
Street, The. *W Cla* 5E 18
Street, The. *Won* 7J 29
Stringer's Av. *Guild* 5F 17
Stringers Common. 6E 16
Stringhams Copse. *Rip* 1D 18
Struan Gdns. *Wok* 6G 5
Stuart Ct. *G'ming* 3A 34
Studland Rd. *Byfl* 4K 7
Sturt Ct. *Guild* 2K 23
Suffield La. *Shack & P'ham* 5A 26
Suffolk Dri. *Guild* 6K 17
Summerhayes Clo. *Wok* 5G 5
Summerhill. *G'ming* 1K 33
Summerhouse Clo. *G'ming* 4K 33
Summerhouse Rd. *G'ming* 4K 33
Summersbury Dri. *Shalf* 5G 29
Summersbury Hall. *Shalf* 5G 29
Summersby Clo. *G'ming* 7B 28
Summers Clo. *Wey* 2K 7
Summers La. *Hurt* 6G 27
Summer's Rd. *G'ming* 7B 28
Sundew Clo. *Light* 2D 2
Sundridge Rd. *Wok* 3J 11
Sun Hill. *Wok* 5C 10
Sunny Side. *Knap* 3H 9
Surrey Ct. *Guild* 4D 22

46 A-Z Guildford & Woking

The representation on the maps of a road, track or footpath is no evidence of the existence of a right of way.

The Grid on this map is the National Grid taken from Ordnance Survey mapping with the permission of the Controller of Her Majesty's Stationery Office.

Copyright of Geographers' A-Z Map Co. Ltd.

No reproduction by any method whatsoever of any part of this publication is permitted without the prior consent of the copyright owners.